Happy Mothers
Day

We Love You Lots!

Missy, Ralph, & Jackie
xo   xo   xo

A
Woman's
Touch

A Woman's Touch

The Fingerprints You Leave Behind

Amy Nappa

Our purpose at Howard Publishing is to:

- *Increase faith* in the hearts of growing Christians
- *Inspire holiness* in the lives of believers
- *Instill hope* in the hearts of struggling people everywhere

Because He's coming again!

A Woman's Touch © 2001 by Amy Nappa
All rights reserved. Printed in the United States of America

Published by Howard Publishing Co., Inc.,
3117 North 7th Street, West Monroe, Louisiana 71291-2227

01 02 03 04 05 06 07 08 09 10   10 9 8 7 6 5 4 3 2 1

Edited by Michele Buckingham
Interior design by Stephanie Denney

Library of Congress Cataloging-in-Publication Data
Nappa, Amy, 1963-
    A woman's touch : the fingerprints you leave behind / Amy Nappa.
        p. cm.
    ISBN 1-58229-159-4
        1. Women—Religious life. I. Title.

BV4527 .N33 2001
248.8'43—dc21   00-054165

A *Woman's Touch* is another creative resource from the authors at Nappaland Communications, Inc. To contact the author of this book, access her Web site (www.Nappaland.com).

To my sisters,
Jill, Jody, and Annette,
whose fingerprints are all
over my life

Contents

Contents

Contents

Chapter Six

HOME, SWEET HOME
Touching Your Family

Chapter Seven

WON'T YOU BE MY NEIGHBOR?
Touching Your Community

Chapter Eight

THE HANDS OF GOD
Touching in and through Your Church

Contents

Chapter Nine

TOUCH AND GO
Random Touches Both Near and Far

Chapter Ten

I'M TOUCHED
Touching Your Own Heart

Chapter One

YOUR FINGERPRINTS ARE ALL OVER THE PLACE!

The Mark of a Woman's Touch

The hands of those I meet are dumbly eloquent to me.
The touch of some hands is an impertinence. I have met people so empty of joy,
that when I clasped their frosty fingertips, it seemed as if
I were shaking hands with a northeast storm. Others there are whose hands
have sunbeams in them, so that their grasp warms my heart.
—Helen Keller, *The Story of My Life*

Evidence

"Clarence! I think I heard something!"

Mrs. Hiller lay in bed, her eyes wide open, and nudged her sleeping husband. Perhaps you've been in a similar situation. You wake in the night hearing a noise or feeling as if something isn't right. That's exactly what happened to Mrs. Hiller. For some reason she woke up, and as she lay there in the dark, she realized something was wrong. Why was it so dark? Why couldn't she see the light they always left burning in the hallway?

She prodded her husband again, and he rolled out of bed to investigate. But as Clarence Hiller reached the head of the stairs, he had an unfortunate rendezvous with a prowler. The two men struggled and fell together down the steps. Gunshots exploded. Mr. Hiller, shot twice, died within moments. At the sound of Mrs. Hiller's screams, the would-be burglar ran.

It is not known whether the intruder took anything from the Hillers' home. But he did leave something of his own at the scene of the crime: his fingerprints. The Hillers' stair rail had been painted just before the break-in, and in the still-drying paint, an imprint was clear.

Later that same night, the local police questioned a parolee named Thomas Jennings. Jennings was injured, had a loaded gun, and was on parole for a previous burglary. His fingerprints also matched those left in the Hiller home. Early the next year he was convicted of the murder of Clarence Hiller.

Sounds like a pretty straightforward, cut-and-dried case, right? Well, it wasn't in 1910, when the crime took place. At that time, the study of fingerprints in relation to solving crimes was relatively new. It had only been six years earlier, at the 1904 St. Louis World's Fair, that experts from Scotland Yard had begun training American officers in the craft of identifying criminals by the fingerprints they'd left behind.

Jennings later appealed to the Supreme Court of Illinois and lost. It was a historic moment. For the first time, the American courts determined that fingerprints were admissible as evidence in a trial.[1]

According to the courts and scientists everywhere, your fingerprints are yours alone. No one else has the same prints as you; even identical twins have different fingerprints. You touch something, and a trace of you is left behind. Whether you realize it or not, tangible evidence exists that you were at a certain location.

The words of Jesus in John 14:11 remind us that Jesus' identity could be traced through the evidence of his actions. When a leper was healed, people knew Jesus had been there. When a hurting heart found forgiveness, there was proof that the voice of Jesus had been heard. The things Jesus did, the miracles he performed, the words he spoke—these were his fingerprints on the world. These touches proved his identity and left evidence that he had touched lives. Even today they are there for us to follow, leading us to the one and only Son of God.

As women, you and I leave fingerprints on the world. No, I'm not talking about hand prints in wet paint, or even messy smudges on windowpanes (although I admit I have a few of those on my kitchen window right now). A woman's touch can leave fingerprints without physical contact of any kind. We leave our impression on the lives of people around us through our words and actions as well as our physical touch. And just as the fingerprints of Thomas Jennings were unique to him, your touch on the lives of others is like the touch of no one else. The "fingerprints" you leave on someone's heart can be traced back to no one but you.

Thomas Jennings's fingerprints revealed that he was a killer. What do your fingerprints reveal about you? What evidence have you left behind—in your home, your church, your community?

Join with me in exploring the impact of a woman's touch. In the following pages, we'll see just how powerful a touch can be. We'll look honestly at our own touches and consider how our words and actions impact those around us. And in the process, we'll learn how to leave touches that will bring blessing and positive change to the hearts and lives of others—as well as ourselves.

Heavenly Father, may the traces I leave behind lead others to you.

Believe me when I say that I am in the Father
and the Father is in me; or at least believe on the evidence
of the miracles themselves.
—John 14:11

The sound of a great name dies like an echo;
the splendor of fame fades into nothing; but the grace of a fine spirit pervades
the places through which it has passed, like the haunting loveliness of mignonette.
—James Thurber in *Collecting Himself:*
James Thurber on Writing and Writers, Humor and Himself

A Permanent Record

"Okay, just relax your fingers and let me do the work."

These were the instructions I received as my fingers were squeezed, smashed onto an ink pad, then rolled over a thick sheet of paper labeled for each of my ten digits. Right thumb, right index, right middle, and so on.

Yes, I was at the local police department being fingerprinted. No, I hadn't committed any crime, and I wasn't under arrest. My husband, Mike, and I were attempting to adopt a child, and an investigation into our background was one of the requirements of the home study. Our fingerprints would be recorded and sent to the Federal Bureau of Investigation, where, through some technical wizardry, the authorities would check to see if our prints were linked to any crimes. So there we were—trying to look respectable and hoping that no one we knew would see us and think we needed to make bail.

After several weeks, what we already knew was confirmed: Our records were clean. (And by about that time the ink had worn off our hands, so they were finally clean too!) But I also knew that from that point on, my fingerprints were on record with the FBI. A permanent record!

Remember your grade-school days? The teacher leaves the room on a quick errand and leaves Alicia (the cute blonde with springy curls) in charge, telling her, "Make sure no one gets out of his or her seat or makes so much as a peep!" Of course the door is barely shut when Steve (also cute but very mischievous) starts shooting bits of eraser at everyone.

Alicia stands up, gives a slit-eyed glare at Steve, and announces, "If you don't stop that, I'll tell the teacher." She pauses for effect, then adds, "And it will go on your *permanent record!*" A gasp is heard throughout the room as everyone turns to see what Steve will do. And because he lives in fear of damage to his permanent record, he gathers the remaining eraser bits in his hand and stows them in his desk. Ah, the power of the permanent record.

Of course, in grade school we never really knew what this "permanent record" was, who made entries into it, or who got to read it. We didn't realize it was simply a file folder in the school office that held our past report cards and notes from teachers regarding our progress (or lack thereof). For most of us, that record is long forgotten, most likely having made its way to a paper shredder or a landfill years ago. Not so permanent after all!

But we do have another kind of record—and this one *is* permanent. It's made up of all the fingerprints we've left, through our words and actions, on the lives of others. It also includes all of the fingerprints others have left on us.

For example, each time I speak to my son, Tony, the impact of my words are recorded on his heart—on his permanent record—and they become a part of my permanent record too. What kind of record will I leave? Will my words be kind, leaving an imprint of love on his heart, or will they be harsh, leaving a permanent red mark of anger?

A woman's touch makes a lasting impression. My own heart bears the imprints of women I have known throughout my life. Their kind words and deeds have become a positive addition to my permanent record. I can trace much of who I am today back to their fingerprints. Over the course of this book, you will hear about many of them.

What about you? What's in your permanent record? As you look over the pages of your "file," do you see a record of people you have touched? Do you recall those who have permanently touched you?

The fingerprints we leave behind on the hearts of others tell who we are, where we have been, and what we have done. They reveal much about our character, our priorities, and even our relationship with God.

In 2 Corinthians 3:3, Paul told the Corinthians that they were a message from Christ, written with the Spirit of God. That message, of course, was one of God's love, acceptance, and forgiveness, written on their hearts for all to read. As we consider our touch upon the lives of others, we need to ask ourselves: What message are we writing?

God's message is love. Ours should be too. Let's write it in permanent ink on everyone we touch!

Lord, you have touched my heart with your love and permanently changed me. Help me to touch others with your love so their lives will be changed as well.

You show that you are a letter from Christ,
the result of our ministry,
written not with ink
but with the Spirit of the living God,
not on tablets of stone
but on tablets of human hearts.
—2 Corinthians 3:3

Cleaning Up after Eve

My husband, my son, and I live in Colorado, and many winter mornings we awake to find a pristine world of dazzling snow. Every surface—the yard, the driveway, the blacktopped street—is concealed under a pure and frosty blanket of white. It's with great excitement that we hurry to tug on our boots, zip up our coats, slide on our gloves, and swathe every remaining part of our bodies in scarves. We want to be the first ones out!

We trek across what was our lawn and carefully fall backward into the perfect white carpet, splaying our limbs to make "snow angels." Even more carefully we struggle to extract ourselves from our designs and turn around to admire our snowy handiwork. We were there. We made our mark!

Before long, of course, we're throwing snowballs, packing mounds of cold, wet stuff into makeshift forts, and adjusting tiny stones to create a face on our snowman. The fresh, white world is quickly gone, and all that's left is a well-trampled, soggy mess.

But at least the scene started out fresh, new—undefiled. Other places sometimes have that same quality. Think of a beach after a receding tide. Fresh sand and untouched seashells await the trample of feet and the burst of sun-soaked activity. Who will be the first one to leave footprints in that smooth, unmarked surface? Who will be the first to find that perfect shell, newly deposited by the lapping waves?

Or consider the appeal of wet cement—a wide, flat, still-damp palette just waiting for the fingertips of a young, mischievous, would-be artist…Should you leave a mark?

Now think of what the world must have been like for the first woman, Eve. Like the scenes above, everything around her was fresh and new, crackling with flawless beauty and infinite possibility. The earth had yet to be touched. Except for Adam, no one had come before her to tamper with perfection.

She and Adam had the privilege of being the first human beings to make their mark on what was a truly undefiled environment. They were the first ones to leave their footprints in the sand. The first ones to see the power and beauty of a waterfall. The first ones to hear the roar of a lion and the song of a bird. The first ones to stop and smell the roses. The first ones to laugh. And as we all know, the first ones to cry.

We tend to forget all the delightful "firsts" Eve got to enjoy in those weeks and months after the Creation because of that other first she's best remembered for: Eve was the first one to sin. And by sinning—by choosing to disobey her Creator and encouraging her husband to follow suit—she left a huge, dark fingerprint on the world, forever marring the beauty of all that God made. We're still reeling from the impact today.

Before Eve's sin, the world was like our miniature models of untouched snow, smooth sand, even wet cement. Everything was perfect and beautiful—until someone came along and left a mark. Of course, some marks are temporary. Snow angels vanish as the temperature rises; footprints in the sand wash away with the next high tide. But the marks we leave on the lives of others cannot be removed.

As I mentioned in the last chapter, our fingerprints leave a lasting impression. Eve's certainly did. Talk about a permanent record! That's why Eve is one of the best examples we can study as we consider the impact of a woman's touch. Certainly, her example is not one we want to emulate, but we can clearly see the impact of her touch on the world. Her actions changed the life of Adam, the lives of her children, and the life of every human being since—you and me included. We are all sinners.

Okay, enough of the bad news. The good news is that even though Eve left a tragic and devastating mark on the world, God has made a provision to actually *erase* those fingerprints. He doesn't just cover the stain of sin with a giant, cosmic whiteout brush. Rather, through the death and resurrection of his son, Jesus Christ, he wipes the slate clean for all those who choose to accept his free gift and believe in his name.

9

This brings up two points to consider. First, it's easy to see that we're each marked with sin. None of us can truly say we've got it all together. Our faults are simply too glaring (at least mine are!). The question is, have you asked Jesus to erase the stain of sin in your life and put his own permanent mark on you? Romans 3:23 reminds us that even though every one of us has sinned, we can be made clean through the gift of grace and redemption offered through Jesus Christ.

Second, you need to ask yourself: Whose lives are being impacted by your touch? Look around this week and take notice. Who sees your frown or smile? Who hears your laugh or growl? Who reads your scathing memo or your note of encouragement? And then consider the effect. Are you, like Eve, dragging down those near to you and causing a chain reaction that drags others down, down, down? Or is that chain reaction like a film of falling dominoes played in reverse—each piece gently pushing up and steadying the one before it?

Through the actions of Eve, the world was marked with a fingerprint of destruction. Through the actions of Jesus Christ, the world can be made clean and new. Through your actions, others can be brought toward Christ and his love—or not. It's up to you.

God of Creation, let us see the world as a fresh place to begin making fingerprints for you.

For God so loved the world
that he gave his one and only Son,
that whoever believes in him
shall not perish but have eternal life.
—John 3:16

In general, dark chocolate is more straightforward,
less playful than milk chocolate.
Those who favor dark chocolate
have little patience with cute candy.
—Sandra Boynton, *Chocolate: The Consuming Passion*

The Chocolate Touch

Remember the story of King Midas, whose greed caused him to wish that everything he touched would turn to gold? At first his new life seemed glorious. All the wealth he could ever want was at his fingertips! But then he touched a rose, and when the newly golden flower lost its scent, he was struck with a twinge of sadness. His melancholy deepened when the bird he touched could no longer sing through its gold beak. But what finally broke the king's heart was when he reached out to touch his precious daughter, and she turned into a statue of gold before his eyes. The moral of the story? There are many things in life more important than money.

I'd like to propose a different sort of story for us here. Instead of "The Midas Touch," our story is called "The Chocolate Touch." In this tale we meet sweet Candace (called "Candy" by those who loved her), who desired chocolate as she desired breath. Now, this was a woman who knew her chocolate. She could discourse for hours about the presentation, snap, and mouth-feel of the various chocolate brands. She could explain at length the myth of "white" chocolate and expound extensively on the emotional fluctuations caused by chocolate's theobromine content. Candy could even tell what kind of filling was in each bonbon or truffle without secretly poking a hole in the bottom or nibbling off a tiny edge. She instinctively knew how to avoid the dreaded nougat and choose the raspberry cream instead.

Perhaps inspired by her Great-Uncle Midas, Candy wished that all she touched would turn to chocolate. To her delight, her wish was granted by the fairy of Chocolateland, Queen Godiva. Candy quickly reached out to a nearby honeysuckle bush, and the leaves turned to chocolate—a delicious garnish for her chocolate cheesecake later that evening, she thought. Next she let her hand fall upon a pecan tree, and immediately she had unlimited access to wonderfully nutty chocolate bark. When a little rabbit crossed her path, she reached out and watched it turn into a solid chunk of chocolaty sweetness. (Didn't you ever wonder how the idea for chocolate Easter bunnies was conceived?)

As the day progressed, Candy touched item after item around her house and neighborhood. "Just think of all the money I'll save on Valentine's Day presents this year!" she gloated as she turned rose after rose into rich chocolate delicacies. Soon her entire home was transformed. Even her car was racing on chocolate syrup fuel in its cocoa-dust-covered engine. Life had never seemed better.

But finally, as with King Midas, Candy's day took a turn for the worse. Her beloved son, Hershey, came home from school and reached up to kiss her. (He wasn't old enough yet to be embarrassed by displays of affection.) At that instant he was forever frozen in time—the world's first Hershey's Kiss. (Well, it might have happened that way!)

The moral of this bittersweet story? No, it's not that I have a corny sense of humor (and an obvious love for chocolate). Rather, it's that we need to be aware of the vast number of touches we make each and every day. Of course, it would be impossible to list every surface our hand touches over a twenty-four-hour period—every doorknob, every handle, every tabletop, every cup or dish; we simply have our fingers on too many things and in too many places.

Yet most of us could track the number of *people* we touch in a day. Think about it. Each encounter, no matter how brief, would count. Your spouse and children, the crossing guard you wave to as you leave for work, the attendant at the gas station, your coworkers, the clerk at the post office, the kid who sells you burgers and fries for dinner, the friend you chat with on the phone or via e-mail—the list might be long, but not impossible to make.

Now think: What is your touch on these lives? Some people you touch consistently—like those in your family or at work. Others you touch here and there—perhaps casual friends or people you volunteer with in your community. And some you touch just once in a while in a random way. Of course, no one turns to gold or chocolate when your hand, your voice, or your influence touches them. But you can still leave a lasting impression that changes the course of their hours, their days, even their lives.

When Jesus walked the earth, people everywhere wanted to touch him and be touched by him. Through his touch, the blind could see and the lame could walk. The sick were healed. And people caught in the snare of sin were set free. No wonder the crowds clamored for the touch of the Savior!

Do people long for *your* touch—or do you sense that they draw back? Is your touch as valuable as gold to your loved ones, as sweet as chocolate? Or is it as hard as nails? Does your touch bring blessing and healing to the people around you—or pain and heartache?

As we continue to explore the impact of a woman's touch, evaluate your own touches each step of the way. Start keeping a mental list of those people you touch on a regular basis, as well as those you touch less frequently. And start thinking about different ways your touch can bring joy, comfort, restoration, and blessing to their lives.

Now, if you'll excuse me, there's a chocolate bar in the cupboard that's calling my name.

Lord, your touch is more precious than gold and sweeter than chocolate. Thank you for touching my life. Now open my eyes to see all those I touch, and help me to make my touch a blessing in their lives.

[God's ordinances] are more precious than gold,
than much pure gold;
they are sweeter than honey,
than honey from the comb.
—Psalm 19:10

It's Laura's fault she broke the plate, it's true.
And that's the tale I have to tell to you.
—Junior Asparagus in *VeggieTales*

Tracing the Traces

No doubt you've seen a few murder mysteries and crime movies in your lifetime. I know I have. Whenever I watch one, I know I can count on the ending wrapping up neatly because the bad guy invariably gets caught. Perhaps he left behind only one fingerprint—let's say, on a drinking glass. But that print is inevitably discovered by the bright young detective, who grabs the glass with a cloth and drops it into a bag so it can be taken back to the police laboratory.

At the lab the glass is quickly examined, a few taps are made into the computer, and within seconds the print has been matched. Up on the computer screen pops the picture of the bad guy, along with a list of his crimes, aliases, and favorite hideouts. The mystery is solved!

In real life, of course, investigations rarely go as smoothly as in the movies. It's not easy for a detective to find fingerprints, much less "capture" them and match them. The fact is, investigators have to train for two or three years to be considered fingerprint experts. And because the training is not cheap, many police forces simply can't afford an expert. They may have staff people with more knowledge about fingerprints than the average Joe, but it's likely the officers have done nothing more than attend a brief seminar or certification course.

And training isn't the only prohibitive expense. The chemicals, light sources, high-tech goggles, cameras, and other devices needed to discover and record fingerprints are costly as well. As a result, these tools are generally reserved for only the most serious crimes. If your bike is stolen, I can assure you the police aren't going to dust your garage for prints!

Another problem: Even if the police department has the time and

14

money to search every crime scene for fingerprints, the investigators still have to struggle to recover identifiable specimens. Small objects (such as the drinking cup in movies) can be taken back to a lab and studied; but if these objects are touched by anything else, no matter how gently, or if they are inadvertently rubbed against the sides of the bag or envelope carrying them, the fragile prints can be damaged.

But let's suppose the detective manages to overcome every obstacle, and he gets the fingerprints. Who's to say the prints will find a match? No listing exists of all the criminals in the world. Computers can only match the recovered prints with ones they have on file—and obviously not everyone has been fingerprinted.

Okay, I know. This is more information about fingerprints than you ever wanted to learn, right? The point is, it takes a lot of hard work to trace fingerprints back to the person who left them. Many crimes are never solved because detectives just can't find the evidence needed to win a conviction. It's as if some criminals vanish without a trace.

Sometimes a woman's fingerprints can be just as elusive. We touch people every day—with our hands, with our voices, with our actions. There's no telling how many prints we leave in our wake. And each touch causes a reaction, whether small or large, in the lives of others. One friend might smile after you give her a gentle squeeze on the shoulder; another might enroll in college after the encouragement you offer over lunch.

Sometimes you can clearly see the effects of your touch. Like in the movies, your fingerprints are found, identified, and traced back to you. More often though—we're in real life, after all—your fingerprints are lost in the shuffle of living, and you don't get credit for your impact.

Don't be discouraged. I devote hours each week to the children's ministry at my church, yet kids aren't running up to me each Sunday shouting, "Great lesson! You changed my life! Thanks for all your work!" But my touch is still there, and I know it's important.

Just because we don't get affirmation and recognition for touching others doesn't mean we should stop reaching out. In fact, *not* getting credit might be more in line with God's Word, which cautions us to avoid the lure of the limelight. Matthew 6:2–4 says that when we do an act of charity, we shouldn't even let our right hand know what our left hand is doing! In other words, don't blow your own horn. Act in secret. Don't worry about getting the credit.

Here's another point to consider. You know how much it means to you when someone *does* come back and say, "You offered me a shoulder to cry on years ago, and it changed my life. Since that time, I've gotten my master's degree and become a family counselor so I can offer to others the kind of compassion and support I got from you that day." (Well, the example may be a little exaggerated, but you get the idea!) We need to remember the people who touch our lives, just as we would want to be remembered. As you evaluate your own touch, think of those who have touched you—and let them know the impact they've had on your life. Take the time to encourage them with a word of thanks, a note, a candy bar (preferably chocolate), or a bouquet of flowers.

Of course, at a crime scene, the detectives are looking for the bad guys. We're not. Let's do our best not to dwell on the touches of the "bad guys" in our lives. Yes, people have hurt us with their words and actions. Their rough fingerprints have left bruises on our hearts. But my intent is not to point us back to those who have hurt us and assign blame.

As we are reminded in Job 4:8, "Those who plow evil and those who sow trouble reap it." Or as we might say today, "What goes around comes around." Let's allow God to deal with the ones who have hurt us. We'll focus *our* energies on touching others with love, not vengeance.

Wouldn't it be neat if we could input the qualities and characteristics of our lives into a computer, tap a few keys, and see pictures pop up of those who've made us who we are today—those who've touched us with the fingerprints of God's love, impacting us forever? I wonder if God has a computer like that in heaven.

All-knowing God, you appreciate the traces we leave behind, even when others do not. Help me to touch others for your glory and not my own.

Sow for yourselves righteousness,
reap the fruit of unfailing love.
—Hosea 10:12

Chapter Two

HE TOUCHED ME

God's Touch on Your Life

Snips and snails and puppy-dog tails,
that's what little boys are made of.
Sugar and spice and everything nice,
that's what little girls are made of.
—traditional rhyme

Sugar and Spice

It's a common phrase: "a woman's touch." We often say that a bare, dark room needs a woman's touch to become cheerful, vibrant, and inviting. A schoolroom full of mischievous, unkempt ruffians needs a woman's touch to be transformed into a happy, groomed, and cohesive class.

But what exactly does it mean—a woman's touch? Is it a gentle touch? A feminine touch? A fragrant touch? Is it similar to a man's touch—or is it something else altogether?

Well, one thing we know: God made women different from men. I've come up with a list of some of those differences in case there's any doubt:

- Women who smoke are 20 to 70 percent more likely to develop lung cancer than men who smoke the same number of cigarettes.[1]

- Women tend to wake from anesthesia more quickly than men.[2]

- Women leave the toilet seat down; men leave it up.

- Women generally stand or sit closer to people than men do.[3]

- Women usually prefer side-by-side conversations while men prefer to talk face to face.[4]

- Men carry briefcases. Women carry diaper bags.

- Women are more skilled at sending and interpreting facial expressions than men are.[5]

- Women are more likely than men to associate touch with personal warmth.[6]

- Men never talk about their stretch marks.

- Men generally handle stressful situations better than women do.[7]

- Women repeatedly score higher on word choice and writing tests, while men score higher on math tests.[8]

- Women breast-feed. Need I say more?

Clearly God has put his fingerprints on both men and women—just not in the same way. Some of our differences are obvious; others are subtler. And while I realize we're talking in generalities—no man or woman lives up to all the stereotypes of his or her gender—we can't get around the fact that God has made us different on purpose. Our bodies are different. We think differently. We react differently in the same situations. It's logical, then, that our touch in the lives of others is going to be different. There *is* something unique about the touch of a woman!

But wait a minute. Women are not all the same, are they? We may have certain common characteristics, but we have plenty of differences too. For example, my friend Sandy is athletic; she's great at coaching kids in a variety of sports. I barely know the difference between a touchdown and a home run. My friend Serina is a gifted artist; she's always drawing the cutest cards and sending them to people who need a lift. I can draw stick figures—which means I keep Hallmark in business on birthdays and holidays.

My sister Jill finishes all the counted cross-stitch projects I start with good intentions. My mom can make a pie out of squash, and I wouldn't even think of trying. My pal Chris approaches a project thinking "big picture," while I'm bogged down in the details.

Women may be similar when you look at them as a large group, but individually we're very different. You, too, are unique. God made you unlike anyone else—not like me, not like your mother, not like any other woman on the face of the earth. That means there's something about *your* touch that's different from mine or the girl's next-door. Your impact on the world is going to be different from anyone else's—man *or* woman.

How so? Take some time today to make a list of the ways in which God has made you unique. How are you different from the men you know—and the women you know? What are your special talents, your particular interests, your strongest characteristics? Keep it positive; don't see only glowing traits in others and flaws in yourself. Think about the gentle, purposeful fingerprints that God has put on you and you alone.

Now, beside each talent or characteristic on your list, write the name of one person you might touch by exercising or displaying this God-given gift. For some items, a name will pop right into your head; for others, you'll need to think for a day or two. But don't give up. Soon you'll be identifying dozens of ways to touch others with the special, one-of-a-kind fingerprints God has placed on you!

So what, after all, is a woman's touch? It's your touch. It's my touch. And it's the touch of God, through us, to a world that's longing for love.

Lord, thank you for caring enough to touch my life in a special way.
Now help me to touch others with your loving fingerprints.

So God created man in his own image,
in the image of God he created him;
male and female he created them.
—Genesis 1:27

Then the Grinch thought of something he hadn't before!
"Maybe Christmas," he thought, "doesn't come from a store.
Maybe Christmas...perhaps...means a little bit more!"
And what happened then...? Well...in Who-ville they say
that the Grinch's small heart grew three sizes that day!
—Dr. Suess, *How the Grinch Stole Christmas*

Mary's Christmas

As I am writing this chapter, the Christmas season is in full swing. I love this time of year with all its festivities, decorations, and excitement, don't you? But maybe you're not reading this in December. If not, just imagine yourself sitting next to a brightly twinkling tree with presents stacked, stockings hung, snow on the windowpanes, and the smell of fresh pine in the air. (If you have to turn up the air conditioning and spray some air freshener to get in the mood, you have my permission to put the book down for a minute.)

True, we all know that Christmas has become a commercialized event, with more and more emphasis placed on spending and material excess each year. Even in our churches, we get caught up in excessive busyness—making the costumes for the children's program, rehearsing over and over with the choir, baking cookies for the caroling party, and on and on—until it becomes difficult to remember the reason we're doing it all.

The reason? Oh, yeah...the manger. The baby Jesus!

You know, we wouldn't have that baby without a woman's touch. A few chapters back we discussed the touch of Eve on the world and the resulting consequences. We said that Eve was one of the best examples of a woman's touch because the impact of that touch, although negative, is crystal-clear for all to see. Fortunately, another woman in the Bible has had a more positive—and just as obvious—impact: Mary, the mother of Jesus.

Mary is the best known of all the women in the Bible. Her name is recognized around the world, and the importance of her role in history is undisputed. Even today more baby girls are named after Mary than any other Bible woman—or any woman at all, for that matter.[9] Now, I'm not out to glorify Mary or help her win a Bible popularity contest. Rather, I want us to examine the touch of this special woman, Mary, and consider what her example means to us today.

Let's start with a quick review of the story. Mary was a young woman with no great social standing or wealth, promised in marriage to a carpenter named Joseph. One day, while she was minding her own business, an angel appeared and said, "Greetings, you who are highly favored! The Lord is with you." Naturally, she was taken aback by this sudden intrusion of a heavenly being into her rather quiet life, so the angel continued, "Do not be afraid, Mary, you have found favor with God."[10] The angel went on to explain that Mary had been chosen to carry the Child of God, to be the mother of the Savior of the world. All of humanity would receive an incredible gift, the angel said—*through her.*

Mary asked the angel a question or two then gave her response: "I am the Lord's servant. May it be to me as you have said."[11] Not "Let me think about this one," or "I'll get back to you on that," or "I'm a bit busy this year…try again another time." Mary simply said yes to God. She willingly gave herself to his plan for her life.

Much has been written or surmised about Mary's feelings in the weeks and months that followed. No doubt she felt the embarrassment of being pregnant without being married. She must have been concerned about the possibility of being divorced by Joseph. (God took care of that, of course.) Then there was the discomfort of traveling to another city for a government-imposed census—nine months pregnant and on the back of a donkey. And there was the misery of delivering her first child (no anesthesia, remember?) in a dirty stable.

We often stop Mary's story there, at the manger. But Jesus didn't begin his public ministry until he was about thirty years old—which means he probably lived in Mary's home for all or most of his years up until then. At least we can be relatively certain that Mary raised her son through his childhood and teenage years, guiding him into manhood. And we know she was with him in the end, a witness to his torturous death and later to his resurrection.

So for Mary, saying yes to God meant much more than a nine-month commitment. What the angel proposed was a daunting, long-term, open-ended task. It would involve great joy—and searing pain.

Yet Mary didn't hesitate. Trusting and obedient, she quickly agreed to God's request. And as a result, redemption was made available to all humanity. Just as Eve left her mark by bringing sin into the world, Mary made her mark by bringing in the Savior.

What can we learn from Mary's example? For one, we shouldn't hesitate to say yes to God! Mary instantly recognized God's touch upon her life. She accepted it and was obedient to fulfill his plan. She didn't try to make a deal; she didn't say, "Well, okay, God. I'll do this for you if you will get me a bigger house with indoor plumbing." She didn't whine about her lot in life. And she didn't try to take credit for her part in the salvation of the world.

Instead, listen to what Mary said:

> My soul glorifies the Lord
>   and my spirit rejoices in God my Savior,
> for he has been mindful
>   of the humble state of his servant.
> From now on all generations will call me blessed,
>   for the Mighty One has done great things for me—
>   holy is his name.
> His mercy extends to those who fear him,
>   from generation to generation.
> He has performed mighty deeds with his arm;
>   he has scattered those who are proud in their inmost thoughts.
> He has brought down rulers from their thrones
>   but has lifted up the humble.
> He has filled the hungry with good things
>   but has sent the rich away empty.
> He has helped his servant Israel,
>   remembering to be merciful
> to Abraham and his descendants forever,
>   even as he said to our fathers.[12]

Mary praised God for choosing her, despite her unworthiness. She realized people would remember her for the rest of time—but only because of what God had done in her life. On and on, she extolled the greatness and the goodness of God. She knew it was God who was wonderful—not her.

Of course, God's touch in Mary's life was unique, and his gift to her has no parallel in all of history. But God has touched *your* life too. He has given you a gift, just as he gave one to Mary.

According to 1 Corinthians 12:6–7, God works differently through different people, but he does work through each person. To *each* of us is given a gift of the Holy Spirit. Your pastor's devout, perfectly coifed wife isn't the only one God has gifted. That incredibly spiritual missionary who eats grubs and sleeps on a cot in the jungle while doing Bible translation isn't the only one God has touched. God has touched *you*. And with that touch comes the responsibility to be obedient, to use the gift he's given—and to give him all the glory.

As I said, it's Christmastime around here. I would be crushed if my son opened his new Rollerblades with glee and then set them aside, never to be used. I would be frustrated if my husband never put to use the new accessories I just bought for his truck. (Ever tried wrapping rubber floor mats?) God must feel the same when he gives us a spiritual gift and then watches us set it aside with the excuse, "I don't have enough time to use this gift," or "I wanted a different one," or "Doesn't it look nice up here on the shelf?"

I want to challenge you to be like Mary—when it comes to God's will for your life, no hesitation; when it comes to his gifts, no excuses. Make a list of the spiritual gifts God has placed in your life. (Not sure what they are? The next section is for you!) Then say for each one, "Yes, Lord! I know this gift is a responsibility, but I'm ready and willing to use it to touch the world for your glory." Commit now to be a grateful recipient of God's great gifts and his overflowing love. And don't be surprised when he touches the world with that love—through you.

Yes, Lord!

Therefore, I urge you, brothers, in view of God's mercy,
to offer your bodies as living sacrifices, holy and pleasing to God—
this is your spiritual act of worship.
—Romans 12:1

God's given me a gift.
I shovel well. I shovel very well.
—The Shoveler in *Mystery Men*

No Surprises

On my thirtieth birthday my husband, Mike, came home with another woman. Okay, so she was the baby-sitter, and he was bringing her home as part of a surprise for me. Mike was stealing me away for the night. He had planned it all behind my back: a delicious dinner at a great restaurant in town, then a long drive to a remote area in the mountains where a tastefully decorated cabin awaited—complete with a rushing river just outside the door and a blazing fire inside. He'd thought of everything: chilled sparkling cider in the refrigerator, a box of chocolates on the table, even a bottle of scented bubble bath beside the tub.

It was a wonderful gift. The problem was, Mike was the only one who knew about it.

I had no idea. I simply knew that Mike was late coming home, dinner was ruined—and I was in no mood for surprises. So when he came in the door with the baby-sitter and told me to pack my bag, I cried in protest, "But I don't know what to pack! I don't know what to wear! I don't want to leave Tony overnight! What's going on?"

Patiently, Mike answered as few questions as possible; he didn't want to ruin the surprise. And eventually I was out the door. The rest of the weekend was a glorious affair, of course. But I still hate surprises, no matter how good they are. I'm the kind of person who wants to know things up front.

Well, there's good news for people like me—and for you too. God has given each of us a gift, and he doesn't intend for it to be a surprise. I'm not talking about the gift of salvation, which is, of course, the greatest gift of all; I'm talking about spiritual gifts.

I began this discussion in the previous section by reminding you that according to the Bible, each Christian has been given at least one spiritual gift. But perhaps you're like me with my birthday surprise; you know something wonderful is ahead, but you don't know what that something is. And once you find out, you're still likely to cry, "But what am I supposed to do with it?"

Entire books have been written about spiritual gifts, so I won't go into great detail here. You might want to visit your local Christian bookstore or church library to find more in-depth studies. But I want to at least touch on this subject because spiritual gifts have a lot to do with a woman's touch.

Basically, spiritual gifts are special abilities or talents God gives to each of us when we become Christians. There are a variety of spiritual gifts, and each one is important. According to the Bible, these include prophecy, evangelism, pastoring, teaching, wisdom, knowledge, faith, healing, exhortation or encouragement, service, giving, leadership, mercy, discernment, speaking in tongues, and interpretation of tongues.[13] This is not an exhaustive list, but you get the idea—there are a lot of them!

It's not God's intention to keep your gift a secret. In a sense, you can open it immediately. But since there is no literal box to unwrap, how can you know what gift or gifts you've been given?

There are a number of ways to determine your spiritual gifts. For one, you can check with your church to see if it offers one of the many spiritual gifts tests that are available. These "tests" are actually inventories with multiple-choice questions to help you narrow down your interests and abilities and relate them to the gifts listed in Scripture. A Christian bookstore might also have one or more of these tests in stock, perhaps as part of a book on spiritual gifts. Taking an inventory is perhaps the easiest and quickest way to begin identifying your gifts.

Another method is to ask yourself: What are the desires of your heart? Do you love to serve others, whether or not you get a reward? You might have the gift of service. Do you find yourself often sending notes of encouragement to lift the spirits of others? Perhaps your gift is exhortation. Of course, this method is not entirely foolproof; our willful hearts often desire the more "glamorous" or attention-grabbing gifts—we may want to be an evangelist, for example, when our real gift is mercy.

Another way to determine your gifts is to ask other Christians who know you well. They might see administrative or leadership abilities you've never noticed in yourself. They might recognize the wisdom you have to offer, or see your great faith.

Another method—the one that relates most to the scope of this book—is to examine the results of your touch on others. Have you observed a young girl following your advice and blossoming? You might have the gift of wisdom. Did your neighbor's frown change to a smile because of the pep talk you offered? You might have the gift of encouragement. Did your coworker decide to give her life to Christ after you explained the gospel to her? You might have the gift of teaching or evangelism.

Sometimes identifying your gift is pretty simple. I love to have others into my home and make them feel valued and welcome, so it's not difficult for me to know I have the gift of hospitality. I also enjoy teaching and have been told numerous times that my lessons are enjoyable, applicable, and easy to understand. Again, it's not hard for me to see I have the gift of teaching.

On the other hand, it may take time and study to recognize the gifts God has placed in your heart. Only after much prayer, Bible study, and input from others did I come to understand I have the gift of wisdom. That one wasn't obvious to me. If your spiritual gifts are not immediately obvious, don't give up. Your gifts are valuable. They're the fingerprints of God pressed uniquely into your heart—and he will use them to touch the world around you. It's important to search them out.

But don't be anxious. God's intent is not to surprise us with our spiritual gifts late in life. ("Okay, I'll finally reveal what's been behind Curtain Number Three for the last twenty-seven years.") It's not his desire to reduce us to begging and pleading to know what they are. God wants us to know how he has touched us, what he has provided for our lives, and the wonderful plan he has for us. He wants to see us obediently and cheerfully using his gifts.

Why? Well, as Romans 12:4–5 reminds us, God has given us our spiritual gifts for a purpose. He has designed his church like a body, and each of us is a part. It doesn't matter what our gifts are; it doesn't matter if we're a heart or a hand, an eye or a toe. We each have an important role. I need to be exercising my spiritual gift and you need to be exercising yours if the body of Christ is going to be strong and effective in the world.

So get that gift out and start using it! The rest of us are depending on you. And God is just waiting to see the smile on your face when you open the box.

Heavenly Father, thank you for giving me one or more spiritual gifts. Open my eyes to see what these gifts are and how to best use them to further spread your touch.

Just as there are many parts to our bodies,
so it is with Christ's body. We are all parts of it,
and it takes every one of us to make it complete,
for we each have different work to do.
So we belong to each other, and each needs all the others.
—Romans 12:4–5 TLB

We are not saviors, but we can help others toward faith.
This means not only loving them while they're still in the mire,
but loving them out of it.
—Elisabeth Elliot in *Quiet Whispers from God's Heart*

Soaking It Up

Recently I found this list of sentences using homographs floating around on the Internet:

He could lead if he would get the lead out.
The farm was used to produce produce.
The dump was so full that it had to refuse more refuse.
The soldier decided to desert in the desert.
This was a good time to present the present.
When shot at, the dove dove into the bushes.
I did not object to the object.
The insurance was invalid for the invalid.
The bandage was wound around the wound.
There was a row among the oarsmen about how to row.
They were too close to the door to close it.
The wind was too strong to wind the sail.
After a number of injections my jaw got number.
Upon seeing the tear in my clothes I shed a tear.
I had to subject the subject to a series of tests.
How can I intimate this to my most intimate friend?

Clever, huh? Obviously, the same words don't always mean the same thing. It depends on the context. Used in one paragraph, a word might have a particular meaning; in another paragraph, it takes on a different flavor. It's the same word, the same spelling—but a totally different impact.

In a similar way, the same touch in the lives of different people is likely to leave very different impressions.

Chapter Two: He Touched Me

Let's go back to our illustration of fingerprints. An interesting thing about fingerprints is that sometimes they're durable, and sometimes they're not. A fingerprint left on a surface such as paper, cardboard, or unfinished wood, if it's kept dry, can last up to forty years. But a fingerprint on a surface such as glass or plastic is much more fragile; just brushing against it will damage the impression.[14] It may be the same touch by the exact same finger. But because the surface is different, one touch has lasting value, while the other quickly passes away.

I think the same is true of a woman's touch. If we consider the lives of others as the "surfaces" we're touching, we can see that some people are like paper, soaking up our touch and making it last. Others are like glass, and our touch is easily damaged, wiped away, and forgotten.

Jesus touched many lives—with different results. One day, when he and his disciples were approaching a village somewhere between Samaria and Galilee, he noticed ten men calling to him from a distance. These men had leprosy, a terrible disease so contagious that victims were required by law to stay far away from other people. But they'd heard about Jesus and his healing power. So without coming too close, they began to call out loudly, "Jesus, Master, have pity on us!"

Jesus saw the men and replied, "Go, show yourselves to the priests." And as the men left, they were healed.[15] They must have seen in an instant that their request had been granted. Can you imagine their incredible joy? Now they could return to their homes and families! They were no longer outcasts! They were free to live again! I can just picture these men leaping, whooping, and dancing with excitement.

What would you do if you were given such an incredible gift? I can imagine myself—after my initial leap and whoop—falling to my knees and crying out in thanks to the person who had granted me a second chance at life. "I owe you my life! Thank you! How can I ever repay you?"

But surprisingly, of the ten men who were healed of leprosy, only one came back to thank Jesus—and he was a Samaritan (a group considered inferior by the Jews of that day). Realizing he had been healed, the Samaritan returned to Jesus, threw himself at Jesus' feet, and began to loudly praise God. He was like paper—soaking up the touch of his Healer. The other nine men, on the other hand, were like glass; the impression of God's touch was all too quickly rubbed off and forgotten.

Notice: It was the same touch on ten, the same healing on ten—but only one response of thanks. Same touch, different hearts—different impact.

You've seen it happen in your own life. Perhaps you're a mother, and you've always done your best to treat your children exactly the same. One turns out to be an honor student headed for an Ivy League school, while the other drops out of high school and is in and out of trouble with the law. Or perhaps you're an employer, and you gave the same bonus to each of your employees last Christmas. Some were thrilled to have the extra cash, while the rest complained, "Is this all?"

You know how it is—you say the same words, yet they mean different things to those hearing them. You offer the same touch, yet it yields different results in different lives. Some people soak up your touch; others wipe it off.

You might look at these situations and get discouraged: "Fine! I just won't do anything nice for anyone!" Yet look back at the example of Jesus. He kept on healing others, he kept on offering salvation—and he kept on being rejected. He still offers salvation today, despite the fact that millions continue to reject him. He keeps on loving without end. He keeps touching us again and again, whether we choose to soak up the touches or wipe them away. Can you be like Jesus and keep on touching lives, even though you may not always get the thanks or the results you hope for?

The answer to that question probably depends upon your answer to this one: How are *you* at soaking up God's touch? His touch in our lives makes a long-lasting, life-changing impact. Through his touch, we find the strength to keep on loving, to keep on giving. So immerse yourself in God's love. Get saturated, drenched, sopping wet. Don't try to wipe it away. The results will be amazing!

Chapter Two: He Touched Me

Gracious Lord, touch me over and over with your love, your joy,
your mercy, your peace. Leave impressions on my heart that cannot
be washed away so that I, in turn, might pass them on to everyone I
touch.

Though grace is shown to the wicked,
they do not learn righteousness;
even in a land of uprightness they go on doing evil
and regard not the majesty of the LORD.
—Isaiah 26:10

What he's been creating, since the first beat of your heart,
is a living, breathing, priceless work of art.
—Steven Curtis Chapman, *Speechless*

God's Fingerprints

Open any women's magazine and you're sure to see thin, beautiful, fashionably dressed models on nearly every page. Their hair is perfect. Their hips are slim. Their makeup is flawless. And, unless you're Cindy Crawford, you think, "I wish I could look like that!"

Apparently that's what thirteen-year-old Emily Chapman was thinking one afternoon as she leafed through some magazines. Scanning the pages, she felt less than perfect, less than gorgeous. She could see that she didn't look like any of the women in the pictures, and she began to cry.

Fortunately, Emily has parents who love her and love God, and they were there that day to dry her tears. Her dad wanted to offer some advice, but he held back. "I was thirteen once," he admits, "but I was never a thirteen-year-old girl, so I can't fully understand all she's going through. Instead," he says, "her mom and I just sat down with her and agreed that life wasn't fair, and we just cried together."

That might have been all that came of that rough afternoon for Emily. But Emily's dad has a special way with words and music. In fact, he's Christian recording artist Steven Curtis Chapman. Chapman wanted to give Emily more than just a hug, and he wanted to communicate his love and God's love without sounding like a preachy dad. So he did what he does best—he wrote a song.

He remembers, "I wanted to say to her somehow, 'Emily, you're a precious treasure. God created you just like you are, to look exactly like you do, and you are precious to Him and precious to us. I don't know what you see when you look in the mirror that you don't like, but what I see is God's fingerprints all over you.'"[16]

And that's how "Fingerprints of God" was written. Reflect on the chorus to this song:

> I can see the fingerprints of God
> When I look at you
> I can see the fingerprints of God
> And I know it's true
> You're a masterpiece
> That all creation quietly applauds
> And you're covered with the fingerprints of God[17]

There's so much truth in these words, and so much that's universal about Emily's situation. We all experience the same feelings. Perhaps, like Emily, we simply don't feel pretty enough. Or maybe we don't feel smart or popular or godly or useful. We don't seem to measure up to the standards of the world, our families, or our friends. Worse, we don't measure up to our own standards either.

Read again the words of the song. Then read Psalm 139:13. God's fingerprints are all over you. He made you to be just who you are. He formed you. He put that nose on your face, that brain in your head, that laugh in your throat, that tear in your eye.

The question is, how will you respond to what God has created? Will you tell God that he made a mistake, that his creation isn't good enough? Will you throw a pity party? Or will you say, "This is what God gave me. This is what he made me to be. His touch is obviously on my life, and I'm going to let that touch pass on from me to others!"

I know. Setting aside our insecurities and fears and trusting that God has a purpose in making us who we are is a tough thing to do—tough, but not impossible.

My youngest sister, Annette, was born with a mental disability. She will never drive a car, own a business, or balance her own bank account. She needs daily help with her personal grooming. She must rely on others for assistance in many aspects of life. Anyone would understand if Annette was despondent, brooding over all the things she'll never do in life. No one would blame her for looking in the mirror and thinking, "God must have passed me by."

Yet, amazingly enough, Annette is the most cheerful person you'll ever meet—ask anyone who knows her. Adults and children alike love to be around her because of her sweet spirit. She has a quick laugh. She's a faithful friend. She has a tender and compassionate heart. She is generous with all she has.

Annette looks in the mirror and thinks, "God has a purpose for me. God made me for a reason. I've got to get out there and do what I'm supposed to do!"

What's holding *you* back? What do you see in the mirror or reflected in your heart that makes you think God has passed you by? Stop dwelling on the negatives! Instead, start praising God for the special fingerprints he's left on you. (Hopefully you've begun to discover what some of those are as you've gone through the chapters in this section.) Get out there and do what you're supposed to do!

God made you the way you are on purpose—and that's just the way he loves you. Why would you want to be any other way?

Father of Creation, you made me in your image to fulfill your purposes. Open my eyes to see how you've touched me and how you can use me—just the way I am.

For you created my inmost being;
you knit me together in my mother's womb.
—Psalm 139:13

Chapter Three

THE TOUCH TREATMENT

Helping the Hurting

Angels of Mercy

The word spread like wildfire through the church community. Nina Brooks had died.

The news was no surprise, but it was a great disappointment. Her illness had been long and exhausting. While Nina had awaited a liver transplant, the church had prayed for her literally around the clock. "Please God, heal our sister, our friend," they cried out. But God has his own ways. Instead of healing Nina on a hospital bed, God's healing took place at the gates of heaven.

Nina first showed signs of illness as a sophomore in college, and her liver began to slowly deteriorate from that point on. She lived with the condition for twenty-three years and, in that time, married and had two children. She worked and cared for her family, enjoying what most would consider a normal life, until the strain on her liver and other organs became too much.

Eventually it was obvious that only two things could save Nina's life: a liver transplant or a miraculous healing by God. So while waiting for a liver, Nina's friends and church family began to pray for a miracle.

Of course, Nina's friends knew they couldn't heal her—only God could. They couldn't assure her that a liver would be made available in time to save her. So they did what they could do to bring comfort and healing to Nina's spirit.

Her sister Wanda appreciated their efforts—especially the prayer support. She shares, "When Nina would have rough times, when we thought she wasn't going to make it, the church held twenty-four-hour prayer vigils, praying every moment of the day."

Wanda recalls many other ways women who were close to Nina ministered to Nina and her family. "There were a number of Nina's close friends, like Gail and Sondra, who were good about being there for her, coming to visit, talking on the phone," Wanda says. "Sondra organized a huge garage sale to help pay for medical expenses. Another friend, Karen, was at the hospital often and was with Nina when she died. These friends were there through the rough times with her."

Another group of women prepared meals, and one who lived near the hospital offered her home to any of Nina's friends or family members who needed a place to stay. The youth group held fund-raisers.

"Nina was crazy about praise songs," Wanda remembers. "She loved praise and worship. Her favorite song was 'Shine Jesus Shine.' Katie, the church worship leader, offered to play the guitar and sing for Nina, but the hospital wouldn't allow it." Instead, Katie made tapes of praise songs so Nina could listen to them on her cassette player. "That really raised her spirits," Wanda recalls.

Colleen, a doctor in the church, was there to answer medical questions. She was able to talk with Nina's doctor, get more detailed information than others could, and then explain what was happening to the family. She was an advocate for Nina's care, insisting that Nina receive attention when she was suffering.

But despite all these efforts, Nina left her earthly home for heaven in 1994, just one month before she would have turned forty-two. She left behind her husband, Jeff, and two children, ages fifteen and eleven. Now these three, along with other family members, were the ones who needed a healing touch.

"If it had not been for my church care group, I don't know how I would have made it through," Wanda admits. "They were there for us. You talk about healing—when a person dies so young, the survivors need that healing touch too."

Meals were brought to family members. A concert was held and dedicated to Nina's memory. The spring after Nina died, the women of the church converged on Jeff's house and did a top-to-bottom spring cleaning: washing windows, scrubbing baseboards, organizing cupboards, and more.

These women were grieving too. They had suffered along with the family during Nina's illness and after her death. But they never stopped doing all they could to bring hope, comfort, and a healing touch—first to Nina, then to Nina's husband and children, sisters, and parents. [1]

Notice that no one person tried to do everything for Nina. Rather, each woman did what she could—whether it was to bring a meal, sing praise songs, talk to doctors, clean her house, pray, or simply be there as a friend. Each of these women offered her gifts, and each gift ministered to Nina and her family in a unique way.

The Bible tells us of countless times Jesus healed those who were sick. Several times he even raised the dead. We don't know why God heals some and not others. What we do know is that we can offer touches of love and mercy to those in need.

Have you experienced this kind of touch on your life? If so, what was the impact it had on you and others?

What touch can you offer?

Lord, thank you for the healing you bring in the midst of pain. Show me how to reach out and touch the sick and hurting in practical ways.

Praise the LORD.
Praise the name of the LORD;
praise him, you servants of the LORD,
you who minister in the house of the LORD,
in the courts of the house of our God.
—Psalm 135:1–2

I will always see this as something God called me to do.
—Joyce Roush, organ donor

The Miracle of Giving

Have you ever donated blood? I had my first experience with a Red Cross blood drive during my senior year in high school. Most of my homeroom class eagerly signed up to give blood. I'd like to say we volunteered out of a noble sense of mission, service, and sacrifice. The truth was, we just wanted to get out of class for half an hour. And besides, they were serving free cookies!

I don't have a fear of needles, so I watched with interest as the phlebotomist located my vein, swabbed my arm with alcohol, inserted a needle, and instructed me to squeeze a rubber ball. All went according to plan; my blood filled the small bag, and soon I was done and heading for the Oreos. That, of course, is when I passed out. But I survived, and I lived to donate blood again (and pass out again...).

Now, I'm the kind who thinks sharing chocolate is a heroic act, so giving blood is fairly grand on my scale. After all, the transaction involves all give and no take (if you don't count the cookies). That's why I was truly amazed when I read about Joyce Roush in the local newspaper.[2] Joyce donated more than blood; she donated one of her organs. While she was still living. To a total stranger!

Here's how it happened. Joyce Roush works as a coordinator of organ donations at the Indiana Organ Procurement Organization. In that position she sees, day in and day out, the need for healthy organs to save the lives of others. Over time, Joyce began to believe God wanted her to do something more that just coordinate the process. Taking to heart one of her favorite scriptures, Matthew 5:16, Joyce decided to "let her light shine" in order to bring glory to God. She volunteered to donate one of her kidneys.

"I really thought in the beginning that this would be no big deal," Joyce relates. "My vision when I volunteered to do this was that thousands of people [must] have done this before me."

Not so. In reality, only one other living person had ever donated an organ to a complete stranger—and that had happened in the same year as Joyce's donation. Yes, people are often willing to donate their organs to suffering family members and loved ones. And yes, sometimes people allow the organs of their deceased family members to be given to strangers. But there's no line of folks waiting breathlessly to give a part of their living body to save the life of someone they don't know. After all, it's a painful and potentially dangerous sacrifice. Who would do it without some strong motivation?

Joyce's motivation was her compelling desire to touch someone with the love of God. Eventually her kidney went to a thirteen-year-old boy named Christopher Bieniek, who showed his gratefulness for this incredible gift by naming Joyce his "other mom." Today he keeps in touch with Joyce via e-mail. She teases him that since she gave him her "smart kidney," she expects good grades on his report card. But most of all, she says, "I just want him to stay healthy."

Amazingly, Joyce doesn't see Christopher as the only one getting a gift out of the deal. "The greatest blessing for me," she explains, "is that for a moment in time, I got to see God's purpose for me and see that manifest. That, for me, has been a miracle."

I will never know how my blood donation back in high school, or any of the donations I've made since then, touched the life of another person. Joyce, however, has the joy of seeing how her touch has truly changed the life of a teenage boy. God used her to bring healing to his body.

By telling Joyce's story, I'm not making a plea for you to go out and donate your blood, your kidney, your bone marrow, or anything else. I'm not even asking you to sign a donor card allowing your organs to be used after your death (though these are great ideas). Instead, I want to encourage you to open your heart to those people you might touch, even if it means a sacrifice on your part.

God might want you to extend his love by offering to baby-sit for the single parent down the street—yes, the one with the runny-nosed kids. He might want you to prepare a hearty meal for that lonely old man who recently lost his wife—and to sit and visit with him while he eats. Who knows, he might even want you to reach out and touch the life of a total stranger in some way you can't imagine right now. Are you willing to set aside your own comfort to touch someone else with God's love?

Joyce Roush's gift brought healing to the life of a young man and, ultimately, glory to God. Your gift of love may not bring physical healing, but it might bring healing to a hurting heart. And that would bring glory to God, too.

God, thank you for the incredible gift you gave through the death of your son. Help me to be willing to sacrifice some of my comfort to bring your healing to the lives of others.

In the same way, let your light shine before men,
that they may see your good deeds
and praise your Father in heaven.
—Matthew 5:16

I enjoy embracing people.
—Thelma Wells

The Hug Line

How much do you know about hugging? Sure, you've hugged some folks in your lifetime. I have too. But let's consider the facts:

- Hugs are not fattening. They don't cause cancer or give you cavities. They're cholesterol-free, and they don't contain any artificial sweeteners or chemical additives.

- Hugs don't require any special instructions, batteries, or tune-ups.

- Hugs are nontaxable, fully returnable, and can be used in all kinds of weather.[3]

- Thelma Wells may hold the world's record for hugging the most people.

You may have heard of Thelma Wells from the popular Women of Faith series of conferences and books. She travels, speaks, and writes on faith and women's issues with Sheila Walsh, Luci Swindoll, Patsy Clairmont, and others. What you may not know is that Thelma worked professionally for years in the fields of teaching and banking. She started her own business in 1980. And she has been a motivational speaker at universities, government agencies, and corporations, speaking on such topics as stress management, self-esteem, and cultural diversity. As you can imagine, a wide variety of people have attended her sessions.

Why do I mention these details? Because everywhere Thelma goes, she has a "hug line." She doesn't just hug people at Christian conferences. She believes in the power of touch and practices it no matter where she is!

"I understand it takes about twelve hugs a day for us to perform at our peak," Thelma explains. "All of my professional life, if people would allow me to hug them, I did. At the end of my seminars—whether it was in government or colleges or universities or wherever—I would say, 'Okay, I enjoy hugging, so if you need a hug today, come by. I won't hug you unless you let me. But come on by.' People seek me out now at conferences—those who have come before. They say, 'All I wanted was that hug.'"

From corporate "suits" to college kids to government officials, people everywhere literally line up for Thelma to hug them. And hug them she does! She realizes that she's doing more than putting her arms around them—she's touching their hearts with something from God.

"There is something about the human touch that not only touches the human body, but touches the spirit and the soul," she says. "And I enjoy embracing people with a godly hug.

"Whenever I'm getting ready to minister—whether it's with a hug, a speech, or a song—I always pray, 'Lord, don't let me do this on my own, but let it be the Holy Spirit that is within me. You move in the way you see fit. I'm just here for you. It's not about me.'"

So what's been the result of all this hugging? Thelma likes to answer that question by telling a story. Here it is in her own words:

There is a wonderful woman—I won't say her name because she's pretty famous—who was at a conference where I was speaking. I didn't know who she was at the time. She seemed to be trying to slip by me without hugging me or saying anything. But I noticed her in the crowd, and she looked like she needed a hug.

So I said, "Excuse me just a minute," to the lady I was talking to, and called out, "Hey you! Going by right there! Come here!"

The woman said, "Me?" and I said, "Yes, you." So she came over and I said, "You know what? You really need a hug." And I hugged her and held her. At first she was reluctant, but then she just got limp. And as I hugged her, I prayed for her, even though I didn't know what I was praying for.

Later I happened to go to an event where this woman was in concert. And I said, "Oh my goodness! That's that lady!" She came up to me and said, "Do you remember me?" I said, "Yes." Then she told me, "The day you called me over to hug me was the lowest day of my life. I was wondering, 'Does anybody care? Does anybody love me?' And that hug saved my life."

Wow! She had had a lot of problems in her life. But she got a hug just in time. So you see, it's essential that we hug people.

The wonderful thing about a woman's touch is that people really want it! We're not trying to get people to eat okra or wear itchy wool undergarments. By offering a loving touch, we're offering something people not only need but want.

Jesus always touched people wherever he went. It's interesting that while he certainly had the power to heal people from afar, over and over we read of him going to where people were and healing them with a physical touch.

I'm not suggesting we have the power to heal physical conditions with our human fingers. But I do believe there's a healing of the spirit that takes place when we touch others. There's a comfort that can't be found anywhere else but in a touch or a hug. Somehow, God's love and power is shared with others through the simplicity of our physical touch.

Have you heard of World Hug Week? It occurs every year during the third week of July. The goal of this week is to encourage everyone to hug three people a day for seven days, and to ask those three people to do the same.[4] But I say, why wait till July? You can start today! Give the people around you the touches they're craving.

Get that hug line going!

Loving Lord, thank you for putting your arms around me and loving me right where I am. Show me someone who needs a hug today, and help me to touch them with your love.

But while he was still a long way off, his father saw him and was filled with compassion for him; he ran to his son, threw his arms around him and kissed him.
—Luke 15:20

46

A girl is innocence playing in the mud, beauty standing on its head,
and motherhood dragging a doll by the foot.
—Allan Beck in
Heaven Sent: The Wonder and Blessing of Every Child

From the Mouths of Babes

"And a little child will lead them." I love this phrase from Isaiah 11:6, which comes in the middle of a wonderful word picture of the coming of Christ.[5] I love its prophetic meaning. But I think this phrase also speaks of another important truth: We have a lot to learn from children.

One young girl in the Bible comes to mind as a wonderful example. She was an Israelite—the Bible doesn't tell us her name—who was stolen from her home and forced into slavery. I cannot imagine the terror this little girl must have felt as she was snatched by a band of raiders, torn from her family, and taken away to a foreign land. We don't know if the rest of her family were taken into slavery or if they were killed by the kidnappers. Either way, life for this little girl was not a pleasant affair.

She was required to serve the wife of a military man named Naaman, the commander of the army of Aram. Naaman was a man of great power and authority; in fact, the raid that ripped the girl from her home might have taken place at his command. But he was sick. He had leprosy, a disease so dreaded and feared that he would soon be forced to leave his home, his position, and his wealth to live out his days as an outcast and die alone.

You would think the young girl would have been happy to hear that her master was dying. How could she have borne any affection for him—the man who so cruelly tore her from her family? Yet the Bible doesn't say that she cursed Naaman or responded to the news with morbid glee.

47

Chapter Three: The Touch Treatment

Instead, she offered a touch of hope. She approached her mistress and said, "If only my master would see the prophet who is in Samaria! He would cure him of his leprosy."[6]

Naaman and his wife could have scoffed at getting advice from a child, but they didn't. Perhaps they were too desperate. The proposal seemed like a long shot—but what else were they going to do? So Naaman traveled to Samaria, found the prophet Elisha, and—to make a long story short—was healed of his leprosy. And in the process, he became a believer in God.[7]

I remember one year in college when I began to suffer from severe back pain. My doctor doped me up on muscle relaxants and pain relievers, and I could do little but sleep for days. Some college students might consider having a good excuse to sleep all day a blessing, but I had recently accepted a summer job as a camp counselor, and I certainly needed to be awake for that! I also needed to be pain-free if I was going to row boats, hike mountain paths, play vigorous games, and otherwise do my job at camp. What a choice: I could either slump around the campground half-comatose, or I could stay permanently grimaced in pain. Which would be worse for a college student placed in charge of an active group of energy-filled, elementary-age kids?

As the time to leave for camp drew nearer, a group of people from my church offered to pray for me to be healed. I figured prayer wouldn't hurt, so I agreed. An announcement was made in church that evening that anyone who wanted to join in prayer for me should meet in a certain room after the service.

When I arrived at the room, I found a handful of adults—and Sylvia. Sylvia was about seven years old, and—I hate to admit it now—I thought she was a bit of a brat. But who was I to kick someone out of a prayer meeting? Obviously *she* thought she should be there.

I sat down, and the others in the room circled around me and put their hands on my shoulder and back. The adults began to pray. To this day I have no idea what they said. But I clearly remember Sylvia's voice piping up to talk to her friend, the Lord: "God, as we lay our hands on Amy, I pray that you will lay your hands on her too." That was it, short and sweet.

The pain remained the next day and the next. I packed my bags and left for camp anyway. But by the time I arrived at the camp-ground—I doubt you'll be surprised—my back felt fine. The pain was gone!

That summer I was able to chase after kids, dodge water balloons, survive on bad food and little sleep, and lead children—just the age of Sylvia—to Jesus. My back pain returned years later, but for those three months I was free of any discomfort.

I don't think for a minute that it was Sylvia who healed me, just as I don't think it was the little Israelite girl who healed Naaman. Only the touch of God can heal us. Yet God obviously used these little girls as instruments in his plan.

We could learn much from them both. They loved God. They were willing to serve. They didn't hesitate, even though others might have considered their advice or presence unwanted. They didn't withhold their touch. God put these young girls in a certain place at a certain time for a purpose, and they were determined to obey, no matter what.

Could the same be said for us grown women?

The slave girl had every reason to withhold help, yet she was eager for another person to know God and his healing power. Sylvia must have had some idea that I didn't find her to be the sweetest child in our church, yet she wanted to pray for me to be well.

Are you holding any grudges that keep you from touching others? Are you too proud to reach out? Are you blocking the healing hand of God with an attitude that says, "I won't help that person because of how she looks…how she acts…how she treats me"?

There's no further mention of the Israelite girl in the Bible. We don't know if she was rewarded for helping Naaman; we don't know if she was ever allowed to return home. We only know that she was an instrument of God who didn't hold a grudge—and healing was the result.

As for Sylvia, she certainly caused me to look again at my attitude toward kids! While she was still a little girl, she caught the bouquet at my wedding; and as the years have passed, she has grown into a beautiful and intelligent woman. It brings me great joy to know that she now touches the lives of children at her church, leading them in songs, games, crafts—and, best of all, to Christ.

Chapter Three: The Touch Treatment

Powerful God, heal me of those hurts that keep me from serving you with a willing and open heart. Help me to be an instrument of your healing touch.

And whoever welcomes a little child
like this in my name welcomes me.
—Matthew 18:5

I try to give to the poor people for love what the rich could get for money.
No, I wouldn't touch a leper for a thousand pounds;
yet I willingly cure him for the love of God.
—Mother Teresa, "Riches"

Touching Jesus

Imagine a busy street in a bustling city. People are milling about, making purchases, chasing after their children, avoiding traffic. Scattered around them, in doorsteps and on street corners, are the homeless, the poor, and the disabled. One of these is a woman so sick that she lacks the strength to kick away the rats biting at her feet. In spite of her pain and misery, no one seems to notice her.

Then a tiny woman stops.

"Can I help you?" she asks. "Can you answer me?"

The sick woman merely moans in response. So, in spite of her small frame, the tiny woman named Agnes picks up the poor lady, carries her to a nearby hospital, and asks for help.

"This woman is dying," is the sharp reply. "It's obvious she has no money, and besides, from the looks of her she's got a highly contagious disease. We aren't touching her. Now get out!"

But Agnes is adamant: "I'm not leaving until someone helps this woman!" She persists stubbornly in her demand until, finally, the hospital staff relents. They admit the sick woman, and Agnes leaves.

Over the days that follow, Agnes cannot rid her mind of this incident. She continues to see poor and dying people all around her in the streets of the city—people no one else seems to see. "These people need a place to die in peace," she thinks to herself, "a place without gnawing rats and gawking eyes. A place that is clean, quiet, and where someone cares. A place where they can know the love of Jesus."

Agnes approaches the city officials and presents her case. "If you will donate a place, I will do the rest," she says. They agree and allow her to use an abandoned building next to a local temple.

Agnes names the building Place of the Pure Heart and gathers other workers to help her. They roam the streets of the city looking for dying people to bring to their house of rest. As if this challenge wasn't enough for Agnes and her friends, trouble erupts in the neighborhood. The people who belong to the temple next-door are angry.

"She's not of our religion!" they fume. "She's going to convert the people she's helping to her own religion. We've got to stop her!" Some of them pelt the workers with stones as they bring in the dying. Others go to the city officials with their righteous concerns, and a police chief is assigned to the case.

When the chief visits Place of the Pure Heart, he sees things that both disgust him and touch his heart. Agnes is caring for a woman with maggots crawling out of open sores, smiling at her and speaking words of love. The other workers are caring for people in similar conditions.

The police chief returns to the angry temple worshipers. "I'll be glad to kick this woman and her friends out of the building," he tells them. "Only before I do, you must get your sisters and mothers to take over the work these women are already doing."

The crowd quietly disperses, dropping their complaint. They keep on with the rock throwing, however, and continue to shout threats at Agnes and her friends.

Time passes, and the tensions continue. Then one day a different sort of crowd gathers outside the Place of the Pure Heart. Agnes goes to investigate.

"He's got cholera!" someone cries out. "Don't go near him! Don't touch him!"

The man before them is drowning in his own vomit, yet no one will help him—no one except Agnes, of course. She takes the man inside, washes him, and puts him into a clean bed, where he soon dies.

This story is true. Now let me fill you in on some of the details. The busy streets were in Calcutta, India. The man with cholera who was given a clean place to die was a respected Hindu priest who belonged to the temple next-door. (He might even have been one of those who'd been tormenting Agnes and her friends.) And because of Agnes's loving touches in his last moments of life, the other Hindus stopped harassing the Place of the Poor Heart.

And Agnes? You and I know her better by the name she was given when she became a nun, Teresa; or as she was named by the Pope's orders when she began her own convent, Mother Teresa.[8]

It's amazing to consider that Mother Teresa gained worldwide recognition by simply taking the words of Jesus to heart and obeying them. She didn't seek fame and fortune. She didn't ask everyone to applaud her and give her glory. She simply obeyed Jesus by feeding the poor and caring for the sick. For this she won the Nobel Peace Prize. Her response to the honor? "I am unworthy."[9] She turned all the attention and gifts that came with the great prize back to the poor and dying, inspiring others to serve beside her.

Mother Teresa touched the bodies of those no one else would. She could not physically heal them. She couldn't offer them expensive medicines and world-class doctors. She simply offered the love of Jesus, and as a result, her touch reverberated around the world.

Take time to consider the exhortations of Mother Teresa to us:

When we touch the sick and needy, we touch the suffering body of Christ.[10]

Someone once told me that not even for a million dollars would they touch a leper. I responded: "Neither would I. If it were a case of money, I would not even do it for two million. On the other hand, I do it gladly for love of God."[11]

Do you know that right where you live, there are many people in the streets? Hundreds come every day to our places, just for a little food, a little human warmth, a smile, a handshake—nothing more. Do you know that?[12]

Since we cannot see Christ, we cannot express our love to Him. But we do see our neighbor, and we can do for him what we would do for Christ if He were visible. Let us be open to God, so that He can use us. Let us put love into action. Let us begin with our family, with our closest neighbors. It is difficult, but that is where our work begins. We are collaborators with Christ.[13]

Now reflect on her words of prayer to Jesus:

Dearest Lord…Though you hide yourself behind the unattractive disguise of the irritable, the exacting, the unreasonable, may I still recognize you, and say: "Jesus, my patient, how sweet it is to serve you."[14]

Mother Teresa saw the face of Jesus in each person she touched. Do you?

Father of Mercy, let me see the beauty of your presence behind the pain of this world. Open my eyes to see the face of Jesus in those in need.

The King will reply, "I tell you the truth, whatever you did for one of the least of these brothers of mine, you did for me."
—Matthew 25:40

Chapter Four

AS GOOD AS NEW

The Touch of Restoration

> *All mothers have their favorite child. It is always the same one:*
> *the one who needs you at the moment. Who needs you for whatever reason—*
> *to cling to, to shout at, to hurt, to hug, to flatter, to reverse charges to,*
> *to unload on—but mostly just to be there.*
> —Erma Bombeck in *1001 Great Stories & Quotes*

That Meddling Mother-in-Law

Did you know archaeologists have recently recovered the diary of Naomi? You remember her—Ruth's mother-in-law? (You can read about her in the Bible, in the Book of Ruth.) The whole diary is too long to reprint here; still, I thought you'd like to take a peek at some of the best parts. The entries skip along through the years, but I think they'll give you a good idea of some of the high points and low points of Naomi's life.

Dear Diary,

Things are not going well here in Judah. We've had no rain for months and months, and there's simply not enough food anymore. The boys, Mahlon and Kilion, are hungry all the time (I can't stand their constant complaining that there's nothing good to eat in the house!), and Elimelech is getting restless. He wants us to move to Moab to find food and a better way of life. I'm not sure that's God's plan for us—and besides, I don't want to leave my friends (except that snobby Lana—I wouldn't miss her for a second). But I have to admit I'm getting a bit hungry myself, and I must obey my husband. Wonder what they're wearing in Moab these days.

Dear Diary,

My life seems to be a mixture of curses and blessings. We moved to Moab and found the food we needed. We even found a bigger house within our budget. But then the most terrible thing happened. Elimelech died! My heart is broken. I guess the saying is true: You never know what a good thing you've got until it's gone.

Now I'm stuck here in a foreign land with a bunch of idol wor-shipers. At least the boys are grown so they can take care of me; I never could have provided for them on my own. Lately they've cheered up my life by marrying two delightful young women, Orpah and Ruth. I know God didn't want us Jews to intermarry with the Moabites, but they're such beautiful, sweet girls. I think they might even be willing to convert. How could I refuse the boys the wives they wanted, especially after all we've been through?

Dear Diary,

Life is again cruel. God truly must be against me. Both Mahlon and Kilion have died, leaving their wives and me with nothing. How can we survive? I've heard there's food in Judah again—and someone said Lana moved away a few years ago. Maybe I'll take my daughters-in-law and go back home. I wonder if anyone there will remember me.

Dear Diary,

We've started our journey, but I just don't think I can take these poor girls away from their mothers. I love them both. Still, I think it's best for them to go back to Moab—it's the only home they've ever known. Besides, how am I going to feed them when we reach Bethlehem? I'm an old woman now!

Dear Diary,

Orpah agreed to go back to Moab, and we said a tearful good-bye. She promised to write. But Ruth, that dear, was stubborn. She insisted on coming along—and she even said she wanted to follow the God of Israel. What a blessing she is to me.

Everyone here in Bethlehem was so excited to see us! But it was embarrassing to come home empty-handed. I left for Moab with such great hopes; now to come back as a widow and without my boys—it's been hard. I told my old friends to call me Mara, which means bitter, instead of Naomi. Every time someone calls me my new name, I'm reminded of the bitterness of my life.

Dear Diary,

Ruth has been such a help to me here in Bethlehem—gathering grain for meals, watching over me, and keeping me company. I wonder if I could find her a good husband in these parts? I'll have to keep my eyes open around town. She's been working in fields that belong to a man named Boaz. I wonder if he's available.

Dear Diary,

My matchmaking instincts are as strong as ever. Under my guidance, Ruth has caught the eye of Boaz. He's such a handsome and godly man—and with a bit of money, too. Imagine my delight when I glanced through some old family albums and realized Boaz is actually a relative! That makes him our protector under the law, and I figure he could purchase our lands or marry Ruth to provide for us and keep our family name alive. Now I've got to make sure no one else steps in to mess up my plan. Hope it all works out…I can just see Ruth and me living in that huge house of his!

Dear Diary,

It's been a long time since I've written. So much has happened! Ruth and Boaz got married. There was a little trouble when another relative stepped forward to claim our land, but God worked it all out—and I didn't even have to meddle! Now Ruth and Boaz have given me a grandson. Little Obed is such a cutie! I get to baby-sit all the time. I almost feel like he's my own. I'm sure there are great things ahead for this precious boy. I never thought I'd see this day.

Okay, so maybe this isn't the *actual* diary of Naomi, and maybe I did take a bit of license with her thoughts and motives. Naomi's story is usually overshadowed by the more romantic events in the life of Ruth. Yet Naomi's touch was important in Ruth's life. She was a mother-in-law who loved her new daughter. Yes, she may have been a little meddlesome—but you can't deny that Naomi always wanted what was best for Ruth.

Naomi's touch was one of restoration. Through Naomi's example, Ruth was introduced to the God of Israel and restored to a relationship with her Creator. With Naomi's guidance, she found a new husband and was restored to a secure and happy life. But Naomi's touch had a broader impact, too—one that opened the door for the restoration of all mankind: Her grandson, Obed, became the grandfather of David, and it was through David's line that Jesus was born.

Naomi couldn't see into the future. In the midst of her sorrow and pain, she had no way of knowing that God was working out an incredible plan that would ultimately lead to the birth of the Savior. All she knew was that she had suffered much heartache. She didn't find joy until late in life. Yet her life touched many others, and God used every twist, turn, and trial for his greater purposes.

We all have heartaches in life. You might be in the midst of one right now. Things aren't going the way you planned. Maybe you've made bad decisions and have brought some of the trouble on yourself. Maybe you did nothing wrong and are simply being knocked around by the course of life in a sinful world. Either way, it hurts. Perhaps you feel like Naomi did, abandoned by God and useless to anyone.

Don't despair. Let Naomi's life remind you that even when life seems hopeless, God is still working in you, still touching you, and still touching others through you. You may not see it now, but you will.

Take time to look back at past disappointments in your life and see if you can recognize God's hand in the midst of them. Can you thank God for the trials that have brought you, ultimately, to a place of fresh joy and a deeper relationship with him? Or is your own relationship with God in need of restoration?

Many thousands of years from now, someone might find *your* diary. Will it be a chronicle of bitterness and disappointment or a tale of joy and triumph over trial? With the advantage of hindsight, the reader will be able to see the persistent, guiding hand of God in your life. But why wait? You can see his hand today—just ask God to open your eyes.

Holy Father, thank you for always being there for me, even when I couldn't see what you were doing. Help me to live so that others see your hand in my life—and may they come to want your touch too.

"I will do whatever you say," Ruth answered.
So she went down to the threshing floor
and did everything her mother-in-law told her to do.
—Ruth 3:5–6

An Eternal Touch

Imagine heading out for a soft drink at the local fast-food restaurant and coming home with eternal life instead! That's sort of what happened to a Samaritan woman who met Jesus at a well two thousand years ago.[1] This was a woman with—to put it delicately—many issues in her life: too many men, too few weddings, and plenty of grist for the town rumor mill. She went to fetch some water at a time of day when she figured the other townswomen would be elsewhere. Why invite trouble? And that's when she ran into the Son of God.

Jesus approached the woman and asked her for a drink. She was taken by surprise, not only because a strange man was speaking to her, but because this man was a Jew. (In those days, Jews refused to associate with the "inferior" Samaritans.) But Jesus struck up a conversation anyway, and before long the woman wasn't thinking about water, men, or the town gossips. She realized that Jesus was the Messiah who had come to save her soul. Immediately she ran to invite others to come and meet him. A crowd gathered, and many Samaritans became believers in Jesus that day.

What a wonderful chain of events: Jesus touched the woman, the woman spread that touch to others, and many were restored to God.

We, too, have been touched by Jesus. Now we have the privilege of spreading that touch to the people around us. How? By keeping our eyes open and our hearts sensitive to the opportunities God places in our lives.

I think of a five-year-old boy who watched his mother being whisked off to the hospital. She was in labor, but little Joey didn't understand. As he followed in another car with his baby-sitter, Joey became frightened that his mother was going to die. And if she did die, he thought, he wanted to be where she was.

Joey expressed his fears to the baby-sitter. Immediately she pulled the car over and, in simple terms he could understand, told him about the reality of heaven and the plan of salvation. Joey's little sister was born the same day Joey was born again.

Years have gone by, and now Joe Gautier is a Christian comedian, sharing the stage with the likes of CeCe Winans, Amy Grant, and Michael W. Smith. In an entertaining way, he spreads the good news of Jesus to audiences everywhere. Because that long-ago baby-sitter, Wilma Wild, didn't hesitate to offer a five-year-old boy a touch of restoration through Christ, Joe now shares that same touch with thousands of others.[2]

I think of a woman I've never met named Miss Taylor. She worked at a candy store my father liked to frequent more than fifty years ago. One day, Miss Taylor invited my father to her church. He went with her. Then he went again and again. Eventually the church's Sunday school teacher led him to Christ.

My father grew up, attended Christian colleges, and became a pastor and seminary professor. Not only has he led others to Jesus, he has trained many to be leaders in their churches and communities so that they, in turn, will touch others with the good news. Along with my mom, he's raised five kids who all follow Jesus and are involved in Christian service. Now we lead others, as our father led us, to the salvation and restoration that's available through Christ.

I think of Cheryl Wong, the children's ministry director at our church, who explains the salvation message over and over to little ones in our congregation. God's touch is passed through Cheryl's words and loving example into the hearts of these children, and they, too, come to know Jesus. Only time will tell how these children will touch others as they grow into adulthood.

The most perfect touch we can offer anyone is the touch of restoration to God. Each of the women in these stories was open to the leading of God in their lives. They invited someone to know Jesus in the simplest way—so simple even a child could understand and respond.

"Will you come to meet this man?" the Samaritan woman asked. "Do you want to know how to go to heaven?" asked Wilma Wild.

"Would you want to come to my church?" asked Miss Taylor. "Do you want to know Jesus?" asks Cheryl Wong. It's not so hard.

You've been touched by Jesus. Now it's your turn. Think of someone you know who needs God's touch of salvation and restoration. What's the question you'll ask that person the next time you meet?

Loving God, you have provided a way for me to be restored to a relationship with you. Give me the courage to share that restoration with the people around me.

Jesus answered her, "If you knew the gift of God
and who it is that asks you for a drink,
you would have asked him
and he would have given you living water."
—John 4:10

Restoring the Temple

Have you even taken an old table or chair and tried to restore it to its original condition? A lot of hard work is involved—sanding, filling in nicks and cracks, staining, more sanding, layering on the varnish. The result is beautiful, but I get tired just thinking about the effort!

I get positively dizzy when I think about what it takes to restore an entire house. Decaying plaster is torn down, old plumbing is replaced, frayed wires are traded for new ones—the work seems overwhelming. The reward (I've been told) is that somewhere in the process, the original beauty of the house begins to shine through. Unblemished hardwood floors are found under several layers of rotted carpeting. A hand-painted mural is discovered behind a length of paneling. The renovations are completed one by one, and finally the job is done. So much effort—but what a great result!

Two books of the Bible, Ezra and Nehemiah, are devoted to restoration projects—but on a much grander scale. It seems the Jews had fallen into a vicious cycle. After times of faith and prosperity, they would be enticed to follow the sinful ways of another nation; they would experience God's corrective punishment, usually in the form of an enemy invasion; and they would return, grateful and humbled, to their worship of the one true God. This pattern was repeated over and over throughout their long history.

We won't go into the lengthy details, but suffice it to say the beautiful temple built in Jerusalem during King Solomon's reign was reduced to shambles by Israel's enemies. In 538 B.C., a group of Jews returned from exile in Babylon to begin the laborious rebuilding process. Their leader was Zerubbabel, and they worked for years to restore the temple despite constant harassment from the local Samaritans. (Think of yourself restoring a table with your two-year-old sticking his fingers in the varnish, crying for a glass of milk when you're in the middle of painting, and running his toy cars over the not-quite-dry surface. That's like Zerubbabel's experience with the Samaritans.)

Over time, the Jews in Jerusalem began to fall away from God again. But another group of Jews returned to the city in 458 B.C., and their leader, Ezra, convinced the nation to restore its faith in God. Little is mentioned of rebuilding, however, until Nehemiah came on the scene fourteen years later. Nehemiah had risen to a high position of service to the king of Babylon, where many Jews still lived in exile. But when he got word that the protective stone walls that had once encircled the city of Jerusalem lay in ruin, he determined to do everything within his power to restore them. (Read about all the work involved in rebuilding the walls in Nehemiah 3–6. It will make your head spin.)

Like Zerubbabel before him, Nehemiah experienced opposition during his restoration effort. But after fifty-two days of hard labor, the project was done. The walls and gates of the city were standing again. The people were secure from their enemies, they had a place to worship, and their faith in God was alive and well.

I've given you a very brief overview of two whole books of the Bible, so you might want to read them yourself to fill in all the details. What's my point? Restoration is a process that involves a lot of work—whether you're restoring a chair, a house, a wall, or something else altogether.

There are two applications I want us to consider. The first relates to our bodies. (No groans please!) Reflect on the work God has put into making us. We're amazing creatures! Just how do our bodies go on working day after day? How is it that we can tell the difference between tastes, sounds, and sensations? How do we learn? How can we be so much alike and yet so different? Sure, you can rattle off scientific explanations for these things, but the truth is, our bodies are complex and wonderful creations.

They are also temples—*temples of the Holy Spirit.* First Corinthians 6:19–20 says, "Do you not know that your body is a temple of the Holy Spirit, who is in you, whom you have received from God? You are not your own; you were bought at a price. Therefore honor God with your body." Just as God resided in the temple in Jerusalem, he now resides in our bodies. That means we need to honor God with our bodies—both in the way we use them (our words and actions) and in the care we give them. That's something to consider the next time we make our way to the refrigerator for another bowl of ice cream!

Are you honoring God with your body? Perhaps your temple needs some restoration—and I'm not talking about plastic surgery. I'm talking about getting back into good physical condition by eating healthful foods, exercising—all that stuff you've been hearing for years but have always let go in one ear and out the other. I'm not condemning you (in fact, I'm reaching for another cookie). I'm just giving you something to think about.

The second application has to do with friendships. Perhaps you can identify with Cathy and Jennifer, two women who hit it off from the moment they first met. They became fast friends and spent countless hours together playing tennis, going to movies, throwing dinner parties, taking road trips, and staying up all night talking, laughing, and crying together.

When Cathy got married, the two women continued spending time together—just not as much. They remained friends, but the friendship wasn't as strong as before.

Then Jennifer got married, and her new husband and Cathy didn't get along. Many tense meetings followed. Hurtful words were spoken between the couples, no apologies were offered, and the wounds between them festered. Within a few years what had been a strong friendship had crumbled into ruins. Both Jennifer and Cathy mourned the loss of their relationship, but neither of them knew what to do to repair it.

Can you think of a relationship you once had that has fallen into disrepair? What would it take to restore the friendship? Restoration, as we've said, involves a lot of hard work. Apologies would have to be laid at the foundation. Hurtful words would have to be stripped away and painted over with a new vocabulary of love and forgiveness. New, stronger bonds would have to replace old ones.

Of course, it's harder to restore something than to build it in the first place. Some friendships, unfortunately, will never be completely restored. And certainly, some relationships are beyond repair. I'm not encouraging you to renew a relationship with someone who has been abusive or destructive in the past. Rather, I'm asking you to think about the friendships that through time, wear, and neglect have fallen by the wayside. Perhaps there's hope to bring life to them again. Only you really know.

But whether you're rebuilding a friendship or getting your temple back in shape, remember this: You're not working on your own. God is in the business of restoration, and he's been at it for a long, long time. We're merely his partners, his apprentices. We're working with a pro! Today open your heart and let God's touch bring restoration to those areas of your life that need repair. Then go and touch others with his restoring love.

Loving Father, thank you for restoring me from a pile of rubble to a temple for your Holy Spirit. Show me those areas of my life that still need restoration, and help me to submit them to your loving, restoring touch.

Restore to me the joy of your salvation
and grant me a willing spirit, to sustain me.
—Psalm 51:12

I invite you to reach out in love to a needy child
and give that little boy or girl something valuable—love and hope.
—Patty Anglin, Acres of Hope

Acres of Hope

Did you ever wonder why, despite all our modern advancements in technology, medicine, and social services, our world is still filled with so much pain? Daily, the news channels blast us with stories of poverty, crime, and disaster. I can't listen to the news without feeling sad. But what breaks my heart the most are stories about children who—through no fault of their own—are subjected to lives of misery.

Consider Brian. By the time he was three, Brian had been physically abused and tortured by his family. He was literally a "wild child," raging in anger at anyone who came near him. It didn't matter if they were trying to help. When a social worker took him somewhere in her car, he kicked, slapped, and bit her while she was at the wheel.

Then there's Cierra. This little girl was born to a thirteen-year-old prostitute who was a drug addict and in juvenile lockup. The mother had been abused herself and knew nothing about caring for a child. Cierra stopped breathing three times as an infant and spent part of her early life in neonatal intensive care.

Serina, Cierra's half sister, was born a year later. She weighed only a few pounds, was addicted to alcohol and crack cocaine, and had an infection that went into her brain. At birth Serina's skin was so transparent that her internal organs were visible beneath it. She had seizures, lesions, and brain inflammation.

Another little girl, Ari, was born with a congenital birth defect affecting her musculoskeletal system. Found in a slum in India by Mother Teresa's Sisters of Mercy, tiny Ari had to be fed with an eyedropper. Her birth defect made it impossible for her to open her mouth more than a fraction of an inch, and by the age of five she weighed only sixteen pounds. She eventually went through thirty-seven corrective surgeries.

Tirzah and her brother, Tyler, were both born prematurely and were addicted to drugs and alcohol. Tyler suffered from hearing loss, mild autism, cerebral palsy, and more. Tirzah's back was scarred from abuse. The children didn't recognize their own names and literally didn't know how to play. They expressed no emotion or awareness of life around them.

Levi weighed four pounds and was almost frozen to death when he was found in a Dumpster by a police officer. He was also legally drunk. Put on life support in a hospital, he tested positive for cocaine and had a host of mental and physical impairments.

Zachary was born strong and healthy but with incompletely formed arms and legs. His parents, due to their cultural beliefs, felt his abnormal form was an evil omen, and they wanted him to die.

The stories of these eight children are enough to bring tears to your eyes. It's tragic enough that one child would have a life of such misery, but literally thousands of children suffer in similar ways throughout the world—even in the United States, where we pride ourselves on being so advanced. What hope do these children have? Where will they find even a shred of joy in life?

Well, if they come to the home of Patty and Harold Anglin, they're sure to find hope, joy, love, laughter, and much more. The Anglins raised seven children of their own, but they didn't stop there. Patty had grown up as a missionary's child in Africa, and she knew all too well about children who were abandoned and without hope. She and Harold decided to open their doors to children with special needs— kids no one else wanted.

For years the Anglins welcomed children on a temporary basis through foster care. But eventually the heart-wrenching pain of having to give up the children after caring for them for months or even years got to be too much.

"This is ridiculous," Patty told her husband. "Why should we constantly have to go through this process of grieving? Maybe we should consider adoption." So they adopted Brian first, and then the seven other children whose stories were very briefly told above. Each child presented a variety of unique challenges. Some, like Serina and Ari, required extensive medical treatment. Many of the children required physical or emotional therapy. They all required constant care and attention. Most of all, they needed to be loved.

As their family grew, the Anglins found they needed more space. Miraculously they were able to purchase a two-hundred-acre farm at a fraction of its value. They named the farm Acres of Hope, and that's just what it is. At Acres of Hope, formerly hopeless children are home-schooled and visited regularly by nurses and therapists. All of their physical needs are met. But best of all, they are touched daily with the hope and love of God.

When Patty shares about these children and their progress over the years, she literally glows with pride. Through prayer, love, and God's grace, each one is thriving. No, the scars do not all heal. There are still daily struggles. But the lives of these kids have been restored as much as is possible on this earth. Now they each have hope—and a future.[3]

In previous chapters, we've talked about restoration. Well, one aspect of restoration is giving back something that was taken— restoring something to its rightful owner. No one would argue that children should grow up with hope, joy, and laughter. When these are stolen from them through abuse and neglect, we all agree it's a tragedy. But who will do something about it? Who will make sure these children are restored to life? How will these kids know the love of God unless someone loves them here on earth first?

I realize that many of us don't have the resources to care for or adopt hurting children. But there are other things we can do to restore hope and joy to these young hearts. You might be in a position to donate money or supplies to a family like the Anglins or to an organization that helps children in your community. They need food, clothing, school supplies, and toiletries like the rest of us. And if the children happen to have special medical needs, you can be sure they need help with doctors' bills and other related expenses.

Or perhaps you could volunteer your time. (There are a few women who have some to spare!) Find your local safe house for abused women and children. The kids there need people to play with them, help them with homework, or just be available to listen while their mothers are looking for jobs or housing.

Do you know of a youngster who is undergoing painful or frightening medical treatments? When that child goes in for surgeries, doctor's visits, or therapy sessions, show up with a special treat. Your small gift of candy, a video, or a new game to play together, or even a funny card, will make the treatment more bearable and restore a bit of joy to the child's life.

In our age of so much knowledge and "enlightenment," many children are still without the hope of Jesus. This isn't God's desire. What's your part in restoring hope?

Kind and loving Father, thank you for women like Patty Anglin who are living examples of your touch of restoration and hope. Show me how I can extend your glorious hope to the children around me— and to any other children you bring my way.

"For I know the plans I have for you," declares the LORD,
"plans to prosper you and not to harm you,
plans to give you hope and a future. Then you will call upon me
and come and pray to me, and I will listen to you.
You will seek me and find me when you seek me with all your heart.
I will be found by you," declares the LORD,
"and will bring you back from captivity.
I will gather you from all the nations
and places where I have banished you," declares the LORD,
"and will bring you back to the place
from which I carried you into exile."
— Jeremiah 29:11–14

'Tis the human touch in this world that counts,
The touch of your hand and mine,
Which means far more to the fainting heart
Than shelter and bread and wine.
—Spencer Michael Free, "The Human Touch"

All Fingers and Thumbs

"The most important day I remember in all my life is the one on which my teacher, Anne Mansfield Sullivan, came to me. I am filled with wonder when I consider the immeasurable contrasts between the two lives which it connects. It was the third day of March, 1887, three months before I was seven years old."

Thus begins the story of Helen Keller.[4] Helen lost her sight and hearing due to illness before she was two. Cut off from the world, she lived in her own reality of darkness and silence and became a wild, sullen child. She communicated pleasure with giggles and unhappiness with kicks and scratches. Then, just before her seventh birthday, Anne Sullivan came into Helen's life. Trained at the Perkins Institution for the Blind in Boston, Anne used her touch—both literally and figuratively—to change Helen's life forever.

Helen wrote about their first meeting: "I felt approaching footsteps. I stretched out my hand as I supposed to my mother. Someone took it, and I was caught up and held close in the arms of her who had come to reveal all things to me, and, more than all things else, to love me."

Over the days that followed, Anne worked tirelessly to teach Helen the basics of communication. After placing a familiar object in Helen's hand, Anne would use finger motions to "spell" the name of the object into her other hand. At first the girl didn't understand the connection between the item and the movements of Anne's fingers upon her palm. Helen copied the movements, but they meant nothing.

Then, one day, everything changed. Anne placed Helen's fingers under a spout of running water and began spelling w-a-t-e-r into her other hand. Suddenly understanding broke like a morning sunrise into Helen's dark world. She knew that the cool, flowing liquid and the w-a-t-e-r being pressed into her palm were the same! "That living word," Helen wrote, "awakened my soul, gave it light, hope, joy, set it free!"

With her touch, Anne Sullivan restored life to Helen Keller—not life in the sense of brain waves and a beating heart, but life in the sense of an understanding of the world and a relationship with the people and things around her. Anne gave Helen the ability to communicate with others, to know their thoughts and make her own thoughts known. The change in Helen's life was nothing short of amazing. Sullivan wrote in her letters, "My heart is singing for joy this morning. A miracle has happened! The light of understanding has shone upon my little pupil's mind, and behold, all things are changed!"[5]

I love this story! It's such a wonderful example of the restorative power of a woman's touch. Because of the touch of one woman, Anne Sullivan, a child cut off from others—from life itself—was restored to the world. Communication was restored. Relationships were restored. And hope was restored—a hope that would characterize Helen Keller for the rest of her life.

Of course, Helen's story is inspirational because it is true. But if you'll indulge me for a minute, I'd like to think of it as an allegory. (I have a vivid imagination!) Helen represents the lost and dying world apart from Jesus—people in darkness, unable to see the light of Christ. Hate and anger abound. Confusion and mistrust are the norm. Anne Sullivan, on the other hand, represents Jesus, coming to restore the light of understanding, love, and trust to their lives. As Helen wrote, Anne "had come to reveal all things," and to love her. How much truer can this be said of Christ!

Anne did not hesitate to get right into Helen's world. She understood Helen's struggle better than others did because she had been partially blinded by an eye infection. She could grasp the misery that was Helen's reality. Jesus, too, got right into our world. He understood our misery because he became a man and lived among us.

If Anne Sullivan hadn't touched Helen Keller's life, both literally and figuratively, the world would never have known the thoughts of this amazing woman, and it would have been our loss. If we don't get involved in the lives of others, they may never experience the joy of knowing Jesus Christ—and that will be a loss of eternal proportions.

As the poem at the beginning of this chapter suggests, sometimes people who are hurting need more than a handout; they need the touch of a loving hand. Certainly that was true in Helen's life. Maybe today is a good day to start touching those around you—literally touching them. Give someone's hand a squeeze. Put your arm around the shoulder of someone who's down. Affectionately rumple a child's hair. Allow your touch to communicate love and restore a bit of joy to their lives. And let your touch open the doors to sharing about your relationship with Jesus—then you'll truly turn on the lights in their darkened world.

Father, give me an understanding of what life is like for those who haven't experienced your touch. Move me to compassion for them, and help me to touch them with your love.

In him was life, and that life was the light of men.
The light shines in the darkness,
but the darkness has not understood it.
—John 1:4–5

A GENTLE TOUCH

The Soft Caress of God's Love

Please don't squeeze the Charmin!
—"Mr. Whipple" in Charmin commercial

The Soft Touch

Remember my story at the beginning of the book about getting fingerprinted in the local police station? During my conversation with the staff woman who pressed my fingers into the ink, I learned that if you touch a surface too hard, your prints can be smudged and become unrecognizable.

"Don't press so hard," she told me. "Roll your finger gently, or you won't get a good print."

Don't press so hard…

There's something to be said for a gentle touch. A touch that's more like a poke or a jab will still leave a print, but not one that's going to be useful to the person being touched. Let me give an example.

Sometime ago, while I was waiting in line at the grocery store to make my purchase, I struck up a conversation with the woman behind me. She had several small children with her, including a newborn. I asked about the age of the baby.

"He's just two weeks old!" she said. "Do you have any children?"

"Yes, I have a son," I told her.

"How old is he?"

"He's nine."

"Oh," she responded. "Are you a single mom?"

I was a caught a bit off guard by her question. I wasn't sure how she deduced that because I had one nine-year-old child I must be a single parent. Her question seemed a little too personal for a casual, grocery-store-line conversation.

"No, I've been married for more than twelve years now," I explained.

"Why don't you have any more children?"

Wow, I thought. *This woman sure is bold! And why is this line taking so long to get moving?* I wanted to say, "None of your business," but the woman seemed genuinely interested. So I answered honestly, "We're unable to have any more children."

"Oh," she said, then pressed on. "Have you thought about adopting?"

Wow and double wow! Bristling under this stranger's pressure, I briefly explained that yes, we had actually tried to adopt several times, but the arrangements had not worked out. *Can I leave my cart right here and just run out of the store?* Then she popped the real question that had been on her mind all along: "Do you go to church?"

This woman was inviting me to visit her church! She was actually trying to reach out to me and lead me to Christ! We talked a little longer, and I learned that she went to a large church in our town; the church had a great ministry to single moms; and she would be glad to call me and make arrangements for us to go to church together. With all the politeness I could muster, I told her I was very involved (*thank-you-very-much!*) in another church and promptly hustled myself through the line, out of the store, and into my car. And locked the doors!

All right, I know. This woman had wonderful intentions. She was trying to strike up a conversation. Find common ground. See where I might be hurting. Offer me a relationship with Christ. But she was pushing much too hard! The fingerprints she left on me were more like a bruise!

Certainly you've met people who are too pushy. They have good intentions, but they cross the line and make you feel uncomfortable. Just this week I read in the paper about a twenty-four-year-old woman who was college educated, never touched drugs, had good friends, and was living a successful life. But because this woman wasn't married, her well-meaning mom got involved. Mom showed pictures of her daughter to men she encountered about town. She tried to fix up her daughter with the sons and nephews of her friends. She even went so far as to place an ad about her daughter in a magazine for singles! Obviously this mother thought she was doing something helpful—but her actions had the unwanted effect of driving her daughter away.[1]

Perhaps you see yourself in these examples. Are you always pushing yourself into the business of others? Do you insist everyone do things your way? Sure you want to help, and your intentions are good, but your poking and pushing could be bruising others.

Sometimes we push without realizing what we're doing. Until my husband, Mike, gently pointed it out, I didn't realize that I was keeping my son from learning how to care for himself by always jumping in to help him when he seemed to struggle with a task. I pulled back, and now Tony can do his own laundry, pack his own school lunch, and complete other tasks about the house. If I'd kept jumping in with my well-meaning, "Here, let me help you," or "Do it my way instead," I'd still be waiting on him hand and foot—and Tony wouldn't be maturing into the capable young man that he is.

Take an honest look at the way you relate to the people around you—your family, your friends, your coworkers. How much are you poking or jabbing instead of gently touching? Do people draw back from you because you push them around instead of guiding them with a gentle hand?

Ephesians 4:2 reminds us to be humble, gentle, and patient, "bearing with one another in love." I prefer how *The Living Bible* phrases that last part: "making allowance for each other's faults because of your love." We all have faults. No one is perfect—especially not you and me! We want others to make allowances for us, to treat us gently. But are we willing to do the same for them?

Instead of pushing others around, God expects you to love them and to make allowances for them. When you use a patient and gentle touch, you show your love—and his.

Gentle Father, thank you for touching my life with a gentle caress instead of a jab. Give me the patience and love to do likewise.

What do you prefer? Shall I come to you with a whip,
or in love and with a gentle spirit?
—1 Corinthians 4:21

Remember there's no such thing as a small act of kindness.
Every act creates a ripple with no logical end.
—Scott Adams, *Dilbert* cartoonist

I Meant to Do That!

A gentle touch is without force, but it's not without intent. There's no use touching someone, however gently, if the only purpose is to feel the palm of your hand on the square of his or her back. No, the point of touching others is to show love—ours and God's. Women who have perfected the gentle touch are always thinking about ways they can quietly let others know they are loved. They know their touches don't have to be spectacular; they simply need to be sincere.

When I left home for college in another state, I lived in the school dormitories. Dorm life had its charms, but it was hard for me to be so far from the ones who loved me—and from their checkbook! I scrimped as much as possible, skipping pizza parties and ice cream outings when I needed to buy soap and toothpaste. On Sunday evenings, when the school didn't serve a meal and students had to fend for themselves, I often wound up eating spoonfuls of peanut butter in my dorm room—or simply stayed hungry until Monday breakfast.

You can imagine my delight the day a messenger delivered a full grocery bag to my dorm room. Inside the sack I found shampoo, laundry soap, deodorant, and other essentials. I was thrilled. Now I wouldn't have to buy these things with my own money. I felt like I'd won the lottery!

The items, it turned out, had been gathered and sent by a woman from my church back home, Linda Lopez. It seems Linda had been thinking of me, and she decided to take action in a practical way. Who would have known that a simple grocery bag would make a poor college student feel so loved? (It also freed me to go out for a burger on Sunday night *and* indulge in a hot fudge sundae!)

Chapter Five: A Gentle Touch

Linda's gift lasted only a few weeks, but her touch on my life was permanent—not just because this memory is forever etched in my mind, but because I now send similar care packages to kids I know who are far from home. I imagine what these college students or short-term missionaries might need to make it through the days and weeks ahead. And as I pack the bag, I add a few fun items like a magazine, a candy bar, a football—things to let them know I not only care about their needs, I want to lift their spirits.

Linda Lopez touched me with kindness, and I am a kinder person because of it. Today my own touches of kindness can be traced, in part, back to her thoughtful, gentle touch.

God's touch in our lives is kind too. We often think of God as powerful, just, and holy. But Romans 2:4 says that it's God's *kindness*—not his power or justice—that leads us to repentance. He has compassion on us. He is sympathetic to our hurts and treats us kindly and gently. And because of this kindness, we want to be closer to him. We want to get our lives right with him.

God's kindness is not arbitrary. He touches us kindly, gently—and with purpose. Our touch, too, should be kind, gentle, and purposeful. By showing love through acts of kindness, we can point people toward the God who is both kindness and love.

Think about someone who has touched your heart by a simple act of kindness. Can you trace how his or her action has become a part of who you are today? Take a few moments to thank that person with a card or a phone call and express how his or her kind touch has made a permanent mark in your life.

Then begin to plan how you can touch someone else with kindness in the coming days. Perhaps a college student you know could use a bag of groceries. Maybe the lonely neighbor down the street would enjoy an evening of board games with you and your kids. Maybe the harried young mother you met at church would be thrilled to have a home-cooked meal delivered to her doorstep around dinnertime.

Begin thinking and planning. Then take action! And don't worry about being spectacular—just be sincere. With your simple, purposeful acts of kindness, you will be touching others with the kindness and love of God.

I Meant to Do That!

✧

Lord, you show me kindness I do not deserve, with the intent of drawing me closer to you. Thank you. Help me to show kindness to others in your name.

Make sure that nobody pays back wrong for wrong,
but always try to be kind to each other and to everyone else.
—1 Thessalonians 5:15

It's easier to get close to someone when there are no hard edges.
—Roman the Teddy Bear in *Teddy Bear Philosophy*

Home on the Range

When we think about the meaning of a gentle touch, certain pictures come to mind: a mother sweetly rocking her baby, a nurse tending to the needs of a hurting patient, a little girl bringing daisies to a neighbor. These certainly are gentle touches of great value. But there is another kind of gentle touch—a touch that may not seem gentle at first because it is neither warm nor fuzzy. Instead, it requires great strength, decisive action, and bold courage.

For an example of this second kind of touch, I'd like us to reflect on a woman in the Bible named Abigail.[2] The events for which she's known occurred thousands of years ago, but they lend themselves to treatment as a good old movie Western (remember my vivid imagination?)…

As you turn on the television, fuzzy black and white images begin to take shape. It's an old movie—a Western, you guess, telling from the rollicking theme song. So you settle back in your rocking chair with a bowl of carrot sticks and a can of Diet Coke (or not), anticipating an enjoyable and restful afternoon.

Quickly the main characters are introduced. There's the cowboy in the white hat, David, and his band of four hundred men who spend their time on the prairie doing good deeds in return for hardtack and beef jerky. Down on the ranch is the obvious bad guy, the wealthy Nabal, who is sullen, rude, irritable, hostile, and grumpy—and since he's not a teenager, there's simply no excuse for his attitude.

Then there's Nabal's wife, a brilliant and beautiful woman named Abigail. You immediately wonder how she ever got hooked up with such a nasty husband. The only possible explanation is that she was forced into the marriage in some matchmaking conspiracy that took place while you were in the kitchen getting another cookie (oops—I mean carrot).

The plot begins to thicken. It's sheep-shearing time at Nabal's ranch, and the ranch hands are having a great time whooping it up, singing, and square-dancing. Then the scene cuts to David and his men, camped out under the stars around a blazing fire. You can almost hear their stomachs growl above the lonely pluck of guitar strings.

David stands to address them. "Men," he says, "we've been out here doin' good for some time now. We've kept an eye on Nabal's sheep and ranch hands, makin' sure they weren't harmed by wolves, stagecoach robbers, or other guys in black hats. I reckon it's time we mention this to ol' Nabal and see if he might send us a few biscuits and a blanket or two."

The men nod and grunt in agreement, their faces glistening in the glow of the campfire. Then David continues, "Jim-Bob, gather up nine other wranglers and head over to Nabal's. Be sure to mind your manners and be polite, offerin' blessin's on his house and all. Then mention our service to him and throw in something about our empty bellies. See if he can help us out a bit."

The camera switches to play out this scene at Nabal's western abode. "Who is this David?" Nabal growls, his squinty eyes flaring. "I never heard o' him or his pa. Why, I'll bet he's some runaway ranch hand. Why should I give him my vittles?" And with that he slams the door in the face of a stunned Jim-Bob and his buddies.

When David hears the report of these insults, he's moved to action. "I can't believe we've been watchin' over this guy all this time and this is the thanks we get," David said. "Grab your weapons, boys!" In an instant the hooves of four hundred horses thunder and kick up clouds of dust as the men ride across the prairie toward Nabal's spread.

Meanwhile, back at the ranch, Abigail gets word of Nabal's rude and unjust treatment of David's men and realizes there will be a showdown at high noon (or sometime soon, at least). "That foolish husband of mine," she sighs. "I have to go clean up after him again." (She doesn't have a Texas accent; she's a college-educated woman from back East.)

Abigail loads up a few cartloads of food, saddles her horse, and rides out to intercept David and his cowboys. The music swells as Abigail, her hair blowing in the breeze, rides toward David and he toward her. Gradually the meadow of wildflowers separating them grows smaller and smaller, and they are finally face to face. Abigail gracefully dismounts her steed and falls before David, who adjusts his Stetson for a better view.

"Accept my humble apologies, good man," Abigail says. "I didn't get to welcome your men myself, and I hope my hospitality is not too late. I've brought out a passel of goodies here. God bless you all for what you've done for our town."

"It's a good thing you found me before I found your fool husband," David responds gruffly. "You've saved the day."

A long scene follows with all the cowboys tearing into the food and Abigail and David sitting to the side, talking about God (this is a Bible-based Western, after all!). Finally, Abigail rides back home. She finds Nabal in a drunken stupor on the sofa, so she pulls off his boots and tucks a blanket around him. Then she takes up her knitting and sits by the fire to wait for him to wake up.

The next morning, a rooster crows, and Nabal awakes with a start. But before he can head out to milk the cows, Abigail tells him what she did the day before to right the wrong he had done. Suddenly Nabal has a heart attack—whether from the shame of knowing that his wife bailed him out once again or the realization that she gave David the bacon he wanted for breakfast, the movie is not clear.

The next thing you see is a calendar with the pages tearing off one by one until it stops on a date ten days later. Abigail is pulling a sheet over the face of Nabal. He's dead. The loyal family cook—he was the one who helped Abigail get all the food together for David and his men—quietly rides across the prairie to get word to David of Nabal's passing. Quickly the scene changes, and the movie closes with David (wearing his best white hat and vest) and Abigail (sidesaddle in a flowing white gown) riding off into the sunset.

The end.

You might be inclined to think Abigail's touch was more heavy-handed than gentle. After all, she did go behind her husband's back when she took the food to David. In reality, Abigail's wise and prudent action corrected a great injustice and prevented certain fighting and bloodshed. Her manner before David was gentle and humble—as well as bold and courageous. She offered herself to David as the scapegoat, asking him to put the blame for her husband's unfairness and lack of hospitality on herself.

Abigail did not hide what she'd done from her husband; she told him about it as soon as he was in a state to remember what she said. Because of her gentle, heroic deed, many lives where saved, and in the end Abigail became David's wife—the wife of the greatest king Israel has ever known.

We may not see dramas such as this one played out in our lives very often. Yet injustices take place around us every day: people left homeless on the street, children abused by their parents, old men and women allowed to suffer alone and forgotten in nursing homes, wives used as punching bags by their husbands. The list could go on and on. Like Abigail, we can touch others by taking bold, courageous action. We have to get involved!

But also like Abigail, we must remember the wisdom of Proverbs 15:1. We can often be more effective with a calm, gentle, self-effacing touch than with an impetuous, blame-throwing, anger-provoking one. Certain injustices may make our blood boil. Still, the best way to address them may be with gentleness and humility, not anger and self-righteousness.

Think about your community, your city. Where are the injustices? Where can you make a difference? How will you proceed?

You don't have to be out picketing, writing letters to the editor, or running for office to change the course of the lives of others. Those can be good things to do in the right circumstances. But the needed touch—the one that will make the difference—might be the one that is gentle and unheralded. Are you ready to take action?

Gentle Lord, open my eyes to the injustices right before me. Show me practical ways I can gently touch others to change their lives.

A gentle answer turns away wrath,
but a harsh word stirs up anger.
—Proverbs 15:1

Mint Condition

My home in Colorado is about an hour's drive from the Celestial Seasonings tea factory. If you're any kind of fan of teas made from flowers, fruits, and other dried items found in nature, you've probably tasted some of their delicious brews.

Most schoolchildren in our area go to the Celestial Seasonings plant for a field trip at one time or another. As a visitor, you're taken first through the gallery where all the original artwork now printed on the tea boxes is displayed. Then you're escorted into an area where everyone dons hair nets, and the factory tour begins. Staying behind the yellow safety lines, you're led past gigantic bundles of dried flowers, spices, and herbs. You catch whiffs of cinnamon, chamomile, and berries as the tour guide explains the process of mixing the herbs and flowers. Finally, you watch machines fill the tea bags and then sort them into colorful boxes, which are then wrapped in plastic and sent on their way to your local supermarket. It's an interesting tour—but I left out the best part!

Along one wall of the plant are two large doors, almost like garage doors. Both of them are tightly sealed. As you approach the first one, the tour guide explains that all of the dark teas are stored in the room behind it. The door is briefly opened, and you're allowed to step inside to breathe in the incredibly rich aroma of the dried leaves. It's a full and comforting smell, deep and warm.

You leave the room reluctantly but with curiosity about the second door that awaits you. It's painted with red and white stripes like a barber's pole, or more accurately, like a candy cane. This is the room where all the peppermint and spearmint is stored. The door is raised, but before you can even step inside your senses are blasted with the strong scent of mint. As you enter the room, your eyes begin to water, your lungs tingle, and your sinuses instantly clear.

The tour group leaves the room rather quickly—the smell is wonderful, but it is also overpowering. That's when the guide explains why these two rooms are sealed off from the rest of the factory. Apparently the dark teas absorb the aromas and flavors of other ingredients to which they're exposed. If they're stored next to a bundle of cinnamon, for example, they'll take on a cinnamon taste. They must be protected in order to retain their flavor. Mint, on the other hand, "infects" all other ingredients. If it isn't kept away from the other herbs and teas, they will quickly take on the aroma and flavor of mint.

Mint is a key ingredient in candy, tea, and various flavorings, of course. Everyone knows it can freshen your breath. But did you know mint has been used to treat cholera, diarrhea, insomnia, abdominal cramping, and nervous disorders? Menthol, which comes from peppermint, is used as a local anesthetic and disinfectant, and it helps people suffering from rheumatism and toothaches.

In some countries, plumbers use peppermint oil to test pipe joints because the strong odor helps them find leaks. Even rat catchers have found a use for mint: Since rats hate the smell, they can be run out of infested buildings and into traps with the aid of peppermint oil–soaked rags.[3]

Clearly mint has more benefits than we usually give it credit for. Still, it's best used in small doses. In large amounts, it's overwhelming.

Our touch on the lives of others should be like mint. While we'd really have to stretch to find a correlation to rat catching, I do think a woman's touch, like mint, can soothe the discomfort and pain in the lives of others. In a sense, our touch can gently "infect" and change their lives for the better—just as mint, when added in small amounts, infuses and complements the flavors of other herbs and teas. As 2 Corinthians 2:14–15 suggests, we can be the fragrance of Christ to those who are lost. We can be like the lingering scent of perfume after the wearer has left the room, almost like a trail leading back to her. Our gentle touch can lead others to the loving touch of Christ.

But remember, there *can* be too much of a good thing. Crushing people with our opinions, advice, and demands can be like the overwhelming power of mint, destroying all other flavors. Our touch should complement and enhance the lives of the people around us—not strong-arm them into being exactly like us.

I know a woman who insists that everything—from making lemonade to teaching Sunday school—should be done her way. Her way is the only way, and all other ideas are crushed under the overbearing weight of her opinions. She is like the overpowering aspect of mint. No wonder people try to avoid her!

I know another woman, however, who gently comes alongside people and teaches them by her example. She's willing to hear their thoughts and concerns, and she might even change her own ways based on their ideas. She never forces herself on others; instead, she makes them feel valuable and appreciated—and somehow a little better for knowing her. She is like the gentle, soothing aspect of mint.

Are you like a touch of mint in your family, your church, your office, your neighborhood? Are people refreshed by your gentle, restrained influence, or are they crushed by your insistent, overpowering ways? Go out and buy a pack of mints today—Tic Tacs, Altoids, Breathsavers, or whatever you like best. Carry them with you in your pocket or purse. Then, every time you put one in your mouth and taste the clear, sharp, refreshing flavor, let it remind you to be like this small dose of mint, touching the lives of others with the soothing refreshment of Christ.

Lord, you are so powerful, yet you treat us with such gentle love. Thank you! Help me to be the "aroma of Christ" to those whose lives need your refreshing touch.

But thanks be to God, who always leads us
in triumphal procession in Christ and through us spreads
everywhere the fragrance of the knowledge of him.
For we are to God the aroma of Christ
among those who are being saved and those who are perishing.
—2 Corinthians 2:14–15

Mercy cannot get in where mercy goes not out.
The outgoing makes way for the incoming.
—George MacDonald in
3000 Quotations from the Writings of George MacDonald

Crushing Personalities

Are you ready? I want you to try a little science experiment. (Humor me—I promise it won't be too hard!) First, put a stopper in the drain of your kitchen sink and fill the sink with several inches of cold water. Next, pour about an inch of water into an empty aluminum soda can and place the can on one of the burners on your stovetop. Turn on the burner and wait for the water inside the can to boil. Let it continue to boil for a minute or so until the can is filled with steam. With tongs (not your fingers!), firmly grasp the soda can. Quickly move to your sink, and with one fast motion turn the can upside-down and plunge it into the water.

What happened? The can appears to have crushed itself! The long scientific explanation has to do with the dynamics of air pressure and the differences between hot air and cold air. The short version is that the hot air expanded (as the can was heated), then the cold air contracted (as the can was plunged into the cold water)—creating a vacuum that caused the sides of the can to collapse into an aluminum heap.

I suppose I could use this illustration to make a point about people who are full of "hot air." But I have something else in mind. I want us to think about how crushing and destructive our touch can be in people's lives if we're not careful. A thoughtless burst of cold air from us can suck all the warmth out of another human being and leave them collapsed in a crumbled heap.

I'm reminded of a passage from Corrie ten Boom's classic book, *The Hiding Place*. Because she and her Dutch family hid Jews from the Nazis during World War II, they were taken away to concentration camps.

89

While imprisoned, Corrie received word that her beloved father had died. Listen as she shares:

> Footsteps were passing on the coconut matting. I ran to the door and pressed my face to the closed pass-through. "Please! Oh please!"
>
> The steps stopped. The shelf dropped open. "What's the matter?"
>
> "Please! I've had bad news—oh please, don't go away!"
>
> "Wait a minute." The footsteps retreated, then returned with a jangle of keys. The cell door opened.
>
> "Here." The young woman handed me a pill with a glass of water. "It's a sedative."
>
> "This letter just came," I explained. "It says that my father—it says my father has died."
>
> The girl stared at me. "Your father!" she said in astonished tones.
>
> I realized how very old and decrepit I must look to this young person. She stood in the doorway a while, obviously embarrassed at my tears. "Whatever happens," she said at last, "you brought it on yourself by breaking the laws!"[4]

How cold and cruel this young woman was! I understand she was under orders, and she was merely following the example of her cruel and ruthless leaders. But couldn't her heart have been stirred to compassion for a woman who'd just lost her father? She had the opportunity to offer gentle words of consolation; instead, she spat out bitter ones, crushing the already damaged spirit of another human being.

Of course, you and I aren't like that! We would never be so harsh and crushing with our words—at least not on purpose. But the reality is, we often are. Do you see yourself in any of the following women?

The Grocery Store Screamer. This woman travels with a slew of children and cannot speak to them in normal tones. From the canned-goods section to the frozen-vegetable aisle, she literally screams at her kids, calling them names, telling them how stupid they are, and threatening them within an inch of their lives—adding an occasional slap to underscore her seriousness. Unfortunately, her actions only guarantee that they'll cry louder than ever.

The Judge. This woman is so holy that she would never be caught in sin. She is loud in her condemnation of the unwed pregnant teenager at church. She makes it clear that the girl will get no shower gift from her and advises the girl's parents to kick their daughter out into the streets. She also condemns anyone who tries to bring new ideas into the church, such as new songs, new outreach activities, or new teaching methods. Her standard response is, "That's not how we've done it in the past!"

The Critic. Whenever this woman visits someone's home, she proceeds to point out all of her hostess's flaws in cooking, cleaning, and child rearing. No casserole is baked to her liking, no window is clear enough, and no child is quiet enough. She's only too happy to explain how everything could be done better. And she always leaves before it's time to wash the dishes.

The Thoughtless Wonder. This woman is so busy thinking about herself that she's oblivious to the suffering of others. If another person loses a job, gets injured in a car accident, miscarries a baby, is forced into bankruptcy, or has another tragedy, she immediately starts spouting pithy phrases about the lack of faith or sin that must be in that person's life. She's a close friend of the Judge.

The Gossip. This woman is as friendly as can be, urging others to confide in her "so I can pray for you." Then she quickly turns around and calls her friends, telling them the confidential tidbit "so you can be praying too." She is amazed when people have hurt feelings because of her blabbing, and she's astounded when they turn the other way when they see her approach.

Okay, these characterizations are exaggerated. But not by much! Any of these women will touch the lives of others and leave a fingerprint—one that crushes the spirits of the recipients. Theirs is a touch that pushes others down and blots out any ray of hope. Just as the soda can was crushed by unseen but very real forces, our harsh actions are both real and effective in crushing hearts.

According to Colossians 3:12–14, God calls us to wrap ourselves in compassion, kindness, humility, gentleness, and patience. We are to be forgiving and loving. None of these words describes the guard at Corrie ten Boom's prison. None describes the Grocery Store Screamer or any of her cohorts. What about you? Do you offer compassion and forgiveness?

Do you treat others with kindness and love? Do you have an attitude of humility? Only when you and I embrace these qualities will our touch be truly gentle, lifting others out of despair and into the hope that comes from a relationship with God.

Gracious Father, open my eyes to see how crushing my actions and attitudes can be to the people around me. Extend your grace to me as I extend it to others.

Therefore, as God's chosen people, holy and dearly loved,
clothe yourselves with compassion, kindness,
humility, gentleness and patience.
Bear with each other and forgive whatever grievances
you may have against one another.
Forgive as the Lord forgave you.
And over all these virtues put on love,
which binds them all together in perfect unity.
—Colossians 3:12–14

Chapter Six

HOME, SWEET HOME

Touching Your Family

Each day of our lives we make deposits
in the memory banks of our children.
—Charles R. Swindoll in
Heaven Sent: The Wonder & Blessing of Every Child

The Good Stuff

Not long ago, my friend Bob took his mother to lunch at a local Italian eatery. They sat down, placed their orders, and began to catch up on the latest family news. While they were talking, the waitress arrived with a large bowl of salad to begin the meal. Bob politely passed the salad to his mother.

"My mom raised me right—ladies first," he explained to me a few days later. But he was surprised when his mother seemed to forget *her* manners.

"When she started putting salad on her plate, I couldn't help but notice that she was digging through the salad bowl, picking out all the good stuff," Bob said. "I couldn't believe it! Of course, I didn't say anything, but inside I was getting more and more annoyed as she removed the tomatoes, the olives, the croutons, and the onions. She was leaving me only the lettuce! I barely managed to keep my composure. Then Mom looked up at me, handed me her plate, and said, 'Here, honey.' She gave me the plate with all the good stuff!"

Bob humbly accepted this gift from his mother and watched her begin to place the remaining lettuce leaves on her own plate. He smiled to himself. He should have known; it was his mother's nature to be giving.

Bob would never tell you this, but he's a giving guy too. He's involved in the lives of people all around our community, giving freely of his time, knowledge, and skill to do what he can to bless others. He doesn't hold back all the good stuff for himself. Instead, he spends many hours helping families work on their cars, remodel their homes, and learn more about God's Word. The giving touch of Bob's mother continues to impact lives through the giving touch of her son.

If you're a mother, you probably weren't surprised that Bob's mom gave him the good-stuff salad. "After all," you're thinking, "that's what mothers do. We give up the good stuff for our kids." You can probably think of countless times when you:

- ❧ Let your child have that last piece of dessert you were actually saving for yourself.

- ❧ Put off a hot bath because your teenager drained the water heater.

- ❧ Ate the crusts of sandwiches or other leftover tidbits because the kids didn't like those parts, and you didn't want to see food go to waste.

- ❧ Missed out on hours or even an entire night of sleep comforting a sick or frightened child.

- ❧ Went without a new pair of shoes so your child could have a warmer coat.

And the list could go on and on! I remember the day when my son, Tony, came home from his friend's house and ran up to give me a big hug. He was about four at the time. "I brought you something!" he proudly announced. I eagerly awaited his gift, then took a deep gulp as he pulled a few Gummy Bears *out of his snow boot*! Precious little boy— he didn't have any pockets in his clothes that day, but he had been thinking about me and wanted to share his snack with me. You can bet I took those slightly soggy, funny-smelling, lint-covered candies from his outstretched hand—and popped them in my mouth! Tony smiled cheerily then bounded off to his room to play. (I, on the other hand, spent the next twenty minutes picking bits of fuzz off my tongue.)

Just this past summer Tony and I went to Catalina Island off the coast of California for a little vacation with some extended family. Tony loves to fish—sort of—and the pier at Catalina is one of his favorite spots. But Tony's definition of fishing is, shall we say, *fishy*. I was the one who baited the hook with pieces of squid, then Tony cast the line into the water. I held the pole while he played nearby with his cousins, then I called him when there was a nibble on the line so he could be the one to reel in the fish. And of course, I was the one who did the scaling and gutting. Sure, he got out of the gross and boring parts—but we both had so much fun that it didn't matter to me one bit. I was simply giving Tony "the good stuff."

Are we mothers martyrs? Not at all! This is simply how we touch our children's lives with love: We *give*. We don't expect a lot of hoopla for our efforts. If fact, we're thrilled when our children honor us with a card once a year on Mother's Day.

Think of a time you watched your son or daughter play hard in a sporting match, sing in a church musical, recite at a spelling bee, or do something else that made you proud. You sat back and beamed, "That's my boy!" or "I'm her mother!" You weren't thinking, "Remember, kid, I didn't sleep for three days when you had your tonsils out!" Mothers don't keep a record of their sacrifices.

They find joy in seeing how their touch is transferred through the lives of their children. They are blessed when they see the best in themselves magnified in their kids. My friend Bob has picked up some of his mother's best traits. What a proud woman she must be!

Tony can be a rough-and-tumble boy, and I know my husband is thrilled every time Tony hits a home run or makes a basket. But I'm thrilled when I see Tony show a gentle side: when he reads or plays a game with his three-year-old cousin; when he's patient with his mentally disabled aunt and helps her figure out how much money she'll need at the movies; when he secretly slips a toy he's purchased with his own money into the locker of a friend who needs a boost. In these moments I see a little bit of myself magnified in Tony. (At least I hope that's me!) I know I've passed on something of my touch through him.

Because of the vast amount of time we'll spend with our children during their lives, they're probably the ones who will be the most influenced, changed, and molded by our touch. So touch carefully! Pour honey into their hearts instead of vinegar. Give them your best side instead of your worst. Bring out the company dishes for them. Write them notes to remind them of your love.

Speak gently to them. Remember, the lips that kiss their wounds can also lay open new heartaches. Compliment them on their strengths and encourage them in their weaknesses. Tell them of your love for God and model that love daily. Let them see you reading your Bible and hear you turning to God in prayer.

After all, you've already received the most sacrificial gift of all time. When God gave us his son, he did so without hesitation or complaint. He gave us "the good stuff" by extending grace and mercy to us instead of judgment. Yes, life can be rough. But in the eternal scope of things, we've already been given more than we'll ever deserve.

The best tribute your children can give you is to grow up to be wise and loving men and women who follow Jesus. Be intentional in touching them. Show them the grace and love God has shown you. They're your legacy to a world that desperately needs his touch.

Loving Father, you have given me all the best of yourself and more. You hold nothing back. Cause me to touch my children in the same giving way.

May your father and mother be glad;
may she who gave you birth rejoice!
—Proverbs 23:25

I wish you were here with me…
I know for a fact if you would have spent a little more time,
I'd be a better person.
—Arnessa, age fifteen, in a letter to her mother in prison

Touch of Grief

Shawn wanted out. Her mother, Beverly, was addicted to crack cocaine and had been stealing money from Shawn and the other kids in the family to support her habit. Shawn wanted to move away from her mother and get on with her life. She had a child of her own to think about. Moving, however, would cost money—and that was something she was a little short on.

So Shawn devised a plan to rob a local Arby's restaurant. She had a .22-caliber rifle and some girlfriends who were willing to help her. There was only one glitch: Shawn was a teenager, and she didn't know how to drive. The problem was quickly resolved when Beverly agreed to drive the getaway car. Mom to the rescue!

Shawn and her mother hit the restaurant at closing time. But as they made their getaway, an observant customer wrote down the car's license-plate number. They were arrested before they even got home. Now mother and daughter are in prison, serving time together.

Michelle and her mother, Mary, are also spending time together behind bars. Mary had been in a gang during Michelle's formative years, and Michelle had witnessed murders, robberies, and other acts of violence before she was fourteen. Mary's touch took hold in her daughter's life, and the two eventually committed a murder together.

Young Starr hated seeing her mother hooked on heroin. She hated watching her get arrested time and time again, hated knowing her mother stole to survive. Starr despised hearing her mother make promises over and over then watching her break them one by one. Yet Starr had no other model to follow, so she copied her mother by drinking, dropping out of school, robbing people, and hanging out with a gang. She, too, ended up in jail.[1]

These sad tales could go on and on. The flip side of my story in the last chapter about Bob and his mother (remember, she gave her son the good-stuff salad?) are stories like these: mothers touching the lives of their children with pain and grief, and their children following in their troubled footsteps—especially their daughters.

It's a known fact that boys whose fathers are involved in crime are more likely to get into trouble with the law themselves. Now more and more studies are looking into the bad habits that mothers are passing on to their daughters. For example, many women who are dependent on welfare come from homes where their mothers were welfare-dependent. Women who use drugs often lead their daughters along the same path of drug abuse. And now we learn that at least 50 percent of the young women behind bars in the United States have mothers who were arrested or incarcerated.[2] Not exactly the kind of motherly touch we hope to have on our kids!

"Well I'm not a criminal," I can hear some of you (hopefully, most of you!) interjecting at this point. "I don't do heroin, I'm not out robbing banks or convenience stores, and I've never been arrested." Same here! But I've used the examples of Shawn, Michelle, and Starr to make a graphic point: Our children are watching us closely, and they don't miss a thing. Even if they don't approve of our actions, they're likely to imitate them.

Just as a gentle, kind, and loving touch can mold our children's lives, so can a harsh, selfish, crushing touch. The negative touches may not be as extreme as the ones we've just considered, but their impact is real, and it remains.

Have you ever asked your child to tell a lie on your behalf ("Just say Mommy's sick and can't come to work")? Has your child watched you keep money that didn't belong to you—an extra ten-dollar bill, perhaps, when a store clerk gave you the wrong change? Do your children see you involved in a sinful lifestyle—maybe getting drunk or high on weekends—then rationalizing, "I'm not hurting anyone," or "Everyone's doing it"?

Are you leading your children astray? Are you bringing a touch of sadness and grief to their lives? These are tough questions, I know, but for some of us, they could be critical.

Sometime ago I heard about a woman who died in a car accident. She was apparently a devoted wife and mother and an active church member. But an autopsy turned up a disturbing fact: The woman had been drinking. She had a high level of alcohol in her blood—a factor that certainly contributed to the crash.

My intent is not to judge this woman. I'm simply sad because I know her actions must have brought great heartache to her family and her community. The fact is, our bad choices and negative actions have a big impact on others—especially our children. Ask yourself: What example are you setting for your kids? What kind of touch are you giving? If you need to clean up your act, now's the time to do it!

We can take heart from God's Word. As Isaiah 49:15–16 says, even if a mother has no compassion for her children, God will not forget them. He has engraved us on the palms of his hands. There is hope! Even if our parents hurt us through harsh words or deeds, we don't have to remain bruised and in pain. We can be made new again through the grace and love of God.

Shawn, Michelle, and Starr can be made new again. They are real people, and it's not too late to pray for them and their families. Perhaps these young women will someday come to know the hopeful, loving touch of Christ in their lives. That's a touch we need, too, if we're going to be the kinds of mothers we want our children to follow.

Dear God, you must grieve each time we touch others with pain. Show me where I am failing you and my children, and help me to change.

Can a mother forget the baby at her breast
and have no compassion on the child she has borne?
Though she may forget, I will not forget you!
See, I have engraved you on the palms of my hands.
—Isaiah 49:15–16

Some pray to marry the man they love,
My prayer will somewhat vary;
I humbly pray to Heaven above
That I love the man I marry.
—Rose Pastor Stokes in *The Columbia Dictionary of Quotations*

Suzie Homemaker?

A friend of mine e-mailed me a great article that has been making the rounds on the Internet. It is purported to be the actual text from a 1950s high-school home-economics book. I've tried to track down its origins, but I have to tell you up-front that no one has been able to verify its source. Still, it seems real enough to me. What do you think? Here are excerpts from the portion that teaches teenage girls how to be successful in married life:

Have dinner ready: Plan ahead, even the night before, to have a delicious meal—on time. This is a way of letting him know that you have been thinking about him and are concerned about his needs. Most men are hungry when they come home, and the prospects of a good meal are part of the warm welcome needed.

Prepare yourself: Take fifteen minutes to rest so you will be refreshed when he arrives. Touch up your makeup, put a ribbon in your hair, and be fresh looking. He has just been with a lot of work-weary people. Be a little gay and a little more interesting. His boring day may need a lift.

Prepare the children: Take a few minutes to wash the children's hands and faces if they are small, comb their hair, and if necessary, change their clothes. They are little treasures, and he would like to see them playing the part.

Minimize the noise: At the time of his arrival, eliminate all noise of washer, dryer, dishwasher, or vacuum. Try to encourage the children to be quiet. Be happy to see him. Greet him with a warm smile.

Make the evening his: Never complain if he does not take you out to dinner or to other places of entertainment; instead, try to understand his world of strain and pressure and his need to be home.

The goal: Try to make your home a place of peace and order where your husband can relax.[3]

Okay, back to the present—and reality! Most women today will read this text and laugh. (I know I did.) Yes, any married man would be glad to come into such a home. In fact, anyone at all would be glad to be there—man or woman!

If you're married, you probably fall short of the 1950s model. (I know I do!) Today's husband often finds himself preparing the dinner, giving the children a bath, and doing much of what was once considered "women's work." His wife is likely to have her own busy schedule—one that doesn't revolve entirely around making him feel like a king.

Still, we need to ask ourselves: What are we doing to touch our husbands' lives on a daily basis? We may not meet our mates at the door every night with, "Welcome home, honey. Here's your paper and slippers. Prop your feet up. Dinner will be ready in ten minutes." But that doesn't mean we should assault them with, "Hey, get it yourself! I've got my own life! Can you tell those kids to shut up?"

I'm amazed at the conversations I have with women (even Christian women) who complain and gossip about their husbands. These conversations often end with something like, "Well, I told him! He didn't wash the dishes, so now he has to sleep on the couch for the rest of the week!" Or, "I just walked out and left him with the kids for the rest of the evening. Let him see how he likes it!"

I realize no man is perfect. But no woman is either. And some marriages clearly could benefit from regular sessions with a pastor or counselor. But these are not excuses to be selfish and rude. We need to start touching our husbands with the grace and love we'd like to receive ourselves.

The truth is, we've already received that grace. When Jesus came into the world, he didn't say, "I'll love you after you show me some respect and get your act together." Instead, his attitude was, "I love you whether you love me back or not." And he continues to love us, even when we make the same mistakes over and over. Shouldn't we approach our spouses the same way?

Yet time and time again we treat other people better than we do our own husbands. If you're like me, you're eager to make a good impression on guests in your home. You clean the house, prepare a delicious meal, dress nicely, and open the door with a smile. (Sound familiar? Think of an old high school textbook...) Why are we willing to make this effort for strangers yet unwilling to offer these same graces to the men we have pledged to love forever?

Understand, I'm not trying to push women into some form of modified slavery. I'm not saying life was better in the 1950s and we should go back to the old ways. But I am saying we need to think about how we are touching the lives of our husbands from day to day. Surely these guys didn't propose to us so we could yell and gripe at them every day for eternity!

Consider how you treated your husband early in your relationship—during your courtship and early months of marriage. If you're like me, you wanted to make him feel special all the time, even at the risk of being called "Suzie Homemaker."

When Mike and I were first married, I got up early to make him breakfast in bed—eggs and bacon one day, pancakes and sausage the next. Finally, Mike said politely, "Thanks, but I don't like to eat much in the morning." I started eating breakfast by myself.

Next I focused my energies on cleaning the apartment and keeping things neat and tidy. This was an exceptional challenge since we, like many newlyweds, were broke and didn't have a functioning vacuum cleaner. I had to pick up all the dust and lint on the dark brown carpet by hand. But Mike didn't seem to notice. Turns out he likes to keep his work area in order, but he doesn't mind if the rest of the house is covered in mold and dust.

I suppose I could have been miffed that Mike wasn't appreciating all the effort I was putting into making him feel special. I could have started to gripe and complain about "that worthless ingrate of a husband." Instead, I decided to find out what *would* make him happy. You see, the things I was doing for him were things that would have made *me* feel special. But Mike and I aren't the same person. He has different things that touch his heart.

I eventually learned that Mike feels loved and valued when I set aside what I'm doing to listen to him, talk to him, and make him my number one priority. To some wives, this might seem a lot easier than keeping the floors scrubbed and baking rich desserts. But for me, stopping to sit down is a challenge. I often catch myself listening for a minute, then butting in with, "The phone's ringing—I'll be right back," or, "Oops! I just remembered there are towels on the clothesline I've got to get in before it rains." And Mike's left feeling that I don't really care.

I have to remind myself that this is the man I'll be spending many, many more years with, and I want to make them happy years for both of us. I can do this best by touching my husband with the gift he cherishes most: my undivided attention.

Your husband married you because he saw something in you that made him feel special. What was that? How can you bring that "something" alive every day? As his wife, you have a unique opportunity to touch and influence him in ways no one else can. By showing God's grace and love, you can actually encourage your spouse to become the man of God he is meant to be.

Commit today to pray for your husband. Let God's touch in your life flow through you to him. I realize you may be tired after a long day's work. The breakfast dishes may still be in the sink, and the kids may need their noses wiped. But whether you're cooking a five-course meal or calling out for pizza, you can begin right now to treat your husband with the love, grace, and forgiveness that will draw him closer to Jesus.

Gracious Father, renew daily the romance in my heart so I can touch the life of my husband with your love.

We love because he first loved us.
—1 John 4:19

My son, I have nothing I can give
But this chance that you may live…
—Yochaved in The Prince of Egypt

A Basket Case

Moses was a great man of God, one of the true patriarchs of our faith. He was also a man who was greatly influenced by the women in his life. Possibly more than any other man in the Bible, he was who he was because of the choices and actions of women—indeed, his very life was saved by a woman's touch.

At the time of Moses' birth, the Israelites lived in Egypt as slaves. Their numbers had grown to such an extent, however, that the Egyptians were nervous about keeping them under control. So the Egyptian pharaoh, or king, decided to kill all the baby boys born to Hebrew mothers. (Just a side note here, since we're talking about a woman's touch. The pharaoh first ordered the Egyptian midwives to do the killing as they presided over the births. But the midwives refused, and God blessed them for it. Pharaoh had to find others to do his dirty work.)

While the pharoah's edict was in effect, a Levite woman named Jochebed gave birth to a boy. She hid the baby from the Egyptian authorities for as long as she could, no doubt having quite a time keeping him quiet and out of sight. You know how loud and persistent an infant's cries can be! But when the boy reached three months old, Jochebed realized she needed another plan. She weaved a basket, coated it with tar to make a tiny boat, and laid her beloved son in it. Then she went down to the Nile River and left the basket bobbing in the reeds.

The baby's older sister, Miriam, hid nearby to see what would happen.

Soon the girl saw the daughter of the pharaoh coming to bathe in the river. Walking along the banks, the princess spied the basket and sent a slave girl to fetch it. Imagine her surprise when she found a crying baby inside! She knew immediately that this was a Hebrew child—one who should have been marked for death. But she had compassion on the tiny boy and decided to let him live.

At that moment Miriam stepped bravely from behind the bushes and offered to find a woman to nurse the baby. Pharaoh's daughter liked the idea, and Miriam ran off to get her mother. Jochebed not only got to see her son live, she ended up being paid to nurse him!

When the boy was older, Pharaoh's daughter named him Moses and raised him in the palace as her own son. And you know the rest of the story: Moses grew up to be God's spokesman and to lead the Israelites to freedom. He became one of the greatest leaders Israel has ever known.

None of this would have happened, however, without the touches of three crucial women in his early years. In a sense, Moses had two mothers: Jochebed and Pharoah's daughter. Both women had compassionate hearts that would not allow them to see a baby killed, and both took a risk in saving his life. Big sister Miriam also played a part by watching over Moses and bravely stepping forward to offer her mother's services in caring for him. (Later she became a leader of the Israelites alongside her brother.) Clearly, Moses was shaped by the hand of God—but God used women to facilitate his work.

A number of years ago my husband and I pursued adoption as a means to growing our family. The arrangements never worked out for us, but I was blessed to get to know several families that had successfully adopted children. One woman in particular made a great impression on me.

Kari and her husband, Jeff, already had three wonderful, healthy children of their own. But something moved in Kari's heart when she heard about the plight of baby girls in China. For a variety of political and cultural reasons, infant girls were being abandoned—either put in orphanages or left to die. Kari knew she couldn't save all of these girls, but she could save one. So she and her family went though the rigors of a home study and began saving every cent they could for the huge expense of adoption. Their efforts paid off, and the day finally came when Kari was able to fly to China and bring Elisabeth home.

A few years later, Kari was moved again with the thought of bringing another child into their home. This time, tiny Abigail came from Korea. And then, after a lengthy search, a dark little bundle in blue named Logan joined their family.

It hasn't been easy. Loving the children—that's easy. But Kari and Jeff have gone through incredible mounds of paperwork. They've paid astronomical fees and expenses. And they've had to endure the stress of knowing that one of the children, after spending years in their family, might be taken from them and returned to the birth parents.

Is it worth it? Kari thinks so. "I know God has a plan. I know God's in control. These kids are my family. It's all in God's hands." I've heard Kari say these words over and over. She's not on a rescue mission. She's not out to save the whole world. She simply knows that God can work through her as she opens her heart to his plans for her life.

I see two issues here. One has to do with the risk that is often involved in doing what's right—in doing the things God has planned for us. Jochebed and Pharaoh's daughter took risks to save Moses. Kari has taken risks in adopting children. Is it worth it? Is it worth the risk to save the life of a child? To add a member to a family? To increase someone's joy?

The second issue has to do with the long-range effects our touch can have on the lives of others. When Moses was still a baby, no one but God knew what was in store for his life. None of the women who were so vital to his staying alive and healthy knew what was ahead. They had no idea what a pivotal role he'd play in history. And who knows today what's in store for Kari's children? Maybe one will be the doctor who discovers a cure for cancer. Maybe one will be the president of the United States. Maybe both will follow in the footsteps of their mother and open their hearts to Jesus.

What are the risks you face in touching and possibly shaping for eternity the life of a child? If you're a parent, you've already come up against some of them. There are risks involved in making the right choices for your children while they're young and in letting them move toward independence as they grow older. Are you willing to do the right thing for their sake?

And what about other kids? You may never adopt, but God can use your touch to improve children's lives—whether they're in your home or not. Is it possible for you to volunteer at a crisis pregnancy center?

Donate funds to a home for unwed mothers? Teach Sunday school at your church? Be a "big sister" to a child living with a single parent?

Your touch can make a big difference in one life—and that one life might grow up to make a big difference in the world. Ask God to show you how to take the first step. It's a risk. But I promise it will be worth it.

Father, the risks are great in loving others. You know that better than any of us! Give me the courage to step out and love those children who are in such great need.

Their bows will strike down the young men;
they will have no mercy on infants
nor will they look with compassion on children.
—Isaiah 13:18

Home is where they want you.
You can more or less assume that you'll be welcome in the end.
—James Taylor, "Home by Another Way"

Soap Operas

Certainly you've heard the old axiom, "Blood is thicker than water." And if you've ever cut yourself, you know this statement is true. But the real point of the phrase has nothing to do with the viscosity of blood; it has to do with relationships. Ties between family members—those related by blood—are meant to be stronger than the ties between acquaintances and friends.

In this chapter we've explored the topic of family relationships. To bring home what I've been trying to say, I want you to try a couple of new science projects. (You didn't know this book was going to make you so smart, did you?) In both experiments, you'll be using water as your medium. Blood is thicker, I know; but the bonds between water molecules are strong enough for our purposes—and a water sample will be a whole lot less painful to collect.

To start, you need two clean sheets of paper and a spray bottle filled with water. Holding one piece of paper in each hand, press the two sheets of paper together. Now let go with your left hand. What happened? The paper from your left hand fell to the floor, correct? Now take the spray bottle, squirt some water on each sheet of paper (you don't have to get them soaking wet, just damp), and try the experiment again. What happened this time? The papers stuck together!

I won't go into all the scientific details (mainly because I don't know all the scientific details), but the reason the papers stuck together is that the attraction between water molecules is very strong. Water sticks to water. Keep that thought in mind while we move on to experiment number two.

For this project you need a bowl of water, a shaker of pepper, and a

109

few drops of liquid dish-washing soap. First, sprinkle a little pepper on the water and watch it float. Stick your index finger in the bowl and move it around a little; the little grains either stick to your finger or stay pretty much spread out across the surface of the water. Now dip your finger into the dish soap, and touch your soapy finger to the water's surface. Did you see that? The pepper grains zoom away from your finger! It's as if they can't wait to get away!

Here's another great scientific explanation: Water molecules stick together, but soap breaks or softens the bonds between them. It wasn't that the pepper grains themselves were repelled by your soapy finger; the water molecules on which they were floating suddenly separated and moved away from one another. Because of the soap, the tight links between the water molecules quickly lost their strength.

We started out saying, "Blood is thicker than water." But perhaps in light of our science projects, we can keep the same meaning but change the phrase to, "Water is tight." (I know, it doesn't have quite the same ring to it. But for our discussion, it works!) Remember, our real topic is relationships. So who are those people with whom you're supposed to be so tight? Your parents, siblings, children, aunts, uncles, cousins, grandparents, and so on—your family. And with today's broader definition of family, you probably can throw in some "step" and "half" relatives, too.

These are the people with whom you have the strongest bonds. You've spent a lot of time with them. You know their quirks and they know yours. You've seen how they've changed over time, both for good and for bad. These are your watertight relationships. You may not have chosen them, but the invisible glue is there, and you can't deny it.

But remember our experiment? Soap weakens the bonds between water molecules. And in family relationships, a little soap can do a lot of damage. That soap might be gossip, sarcasm, rudeness, taking people for granted, jealousy, or pettiness—just for starters. I'm sure you can add to the list. These soapy troublemakers put a wedge in relationships and nudge people apart. They weaken the bonds of family and make it difficult for family members to stick together again.

Sometimes the smallest things can put that soapy finger into relationships. One woman snaps at her sister because she bought a desk just like her own—a grown woman essentially whining, "She's copying me!"

That's soap weakening the bonds. Another woman, playing favorites with her children, tells them that she's leaving more money in her will to some than to others. *Soap and more soap!* A sister tells lies to her siblings —just little white lies, she thinks—so she'll look better in their eyes. But they know she's lying, and their trust in her lessens each year. *Soap bubbles bursting here.*

Two aunts can't be in the same room without making snide remarks about one another. When confronted, they take a shocked tone, saying, "I was just joking. Can't you take a joke?" *The suds are thick, the water thin.* At the family reunion, a crowd quickly gathers when Grandma says, "Did you hear the latest about Uncle Homer?" *The foam is leaving scum in the sink.*

The Old Testament tells many stories of families torn apart because of the soapy fingers of women. Isaac's wife, Rebekah, played favorites with her sons and lied to her husband to make sure her favorite son, Jacob, got the best inheritance. Later Jacob fell in love with the beautiful Rachel, but Rachel's father and older sister, Leah, tricked him into marrying Leah first. Is it any wonder these two sisters never got along? Even their children hated each other.

But Leah wasn't the only sister with soap on her hands. Sometime later, Rachel stole a household item from her father and lied to everyone about it, adding to the deep distrust within the family. And I'm just getting started in the Book of Genesis! The stories of these families are more twisted than the plots of many of today's soap operas—largely because of the soapy touches of women who helped weaken what should have been strong family bonds. Of all the women in the Bible, these are the ones you don't want to emulate!

A woman's touch can build up her family or tear it apart. Little words and actions can encourage, bring joy, and pull a family together. They can also destroy, bring pain, and push people apart. It's easy to put the blame on others in the family, but we need to look at our own soapy hands and take responsibility for the fingerprints we're leaving in our wake.

Think about the way you touch the members of your own family. Is there soap on your hands? Is your family stronger because of your touch, or have you allowed your own feelings of jealousy, anger, or distrust to weaken the bonds?

Wash your hands today and rinse them well. Get the soap off before you start touching your family members—and take some time to pour the cool, soothing water of forgiveness over any wounds that are there. With the help and the grace of God, those bonds can grow tight again.

Father, thank you for giving us the ability to make our families stronger. Help me to tighten the bonds of my family instead of tearing them apart.

Finally, all of you, live in harmony with one another;
be sympathetic, love as brothers, be compassionate and humble.
Do not repay evil with evil or insult with insult,
but with blessing, because to this you were called
so that you may inherit a blessing.
—1 Peter 3:8–9

Chapter Seven

WON'T YOU BE MY NEIGHBOR?

Touching Your Community

Love is not communicated in the big event
but in the small acts of kindness.
—Richard Foster in *Leadership*

Kool-Aid Moms

"I woke up around six in the morning with pain in my arm," my friend Rene remembers. "My mom took me to the hospital emergency room, and as we were going in, Nellie and her mom, Mrs. Aste, were leaving. Nellie had on a huge neck and back brace. Some of her vertebrae had been crushed. As soon as I saw her, I started crying."[1]

Rene and Nellie were both at the hospital for the same reason. They'd been in a car accident together the night before. A teenage driver who'd had a few beers too many sent their car rolling once, twice, three times down a Colorado mountainside. No one was killed, but there had been serious injuries. Nellie had been treated overnight and was now being released. But Rene hadn't gone straight to the hospital from the scene. Instead, she'd been taken to jail, where she was held and then released on bail. You see, she was the driver.

Now she had to face her friend—and perhaps even more difficult, her friend's mother, Geri Aste.

Let's back up a year or two. Rene had first come into the Aste home through her friendship with Geri's kids. Right away, Rene noticed Mrs. Aste's loving attitude. "I remember her warmth, her smile, and her laugh," Rene says. The atmosphere seemed unusual to Rene. Her parents were not Christians, and there was little laughter or affection in her own home. She knew something was different about Mrs. Aste. Rene figured it had something to do with God.

Rene began attending church with the Astes and eventually became a Christian. But her lifestyle didn't change much. After asking Jesus to come into her life, "I think I went out and partied the next day!" Rene admits. "And I wasn't the kind of friend I would now allow my own kids to have. Nellie and I would lie to our parents and sneak out to parties. I wasn't a good influence on Mrs. Aste's children."

In spite of her faults, Rene was welcomed again and again into the Aste home. But then came the car accident. Rene was overcome with guilt and embarrassment. She'd put Nellie's life in danger and caused her friend serious injury.

Geri Aste could have yelled and screamed at Rene in the hospital that night. She could have turned a cold shoulder to her and walked away. Instead, she touched her. "Mrs. Aste walked over to me and hugged me," Rene remembers. She put her arms around Rene and offered her forgiveness.

A woman's touch can speak volumes.

Nearly twenty years have passed since that car accident. Rene is married (Nellie was in the wedding) and the mother of two girls. She's active in church, reaching out weekly to young girls as a teacher, mentor, and Christian role model. And when Rene's father recently passed away, Mrs. Aste was there again to offer a hug.

Consider the children who come into your home. They could be the friends of your own children, neighborhood kids who stop by to visit, nieces, nephews, or grandchildren. Whoever they are, they need to know the love of Jesus—and you might be the only one who will show it to them.

Just as Geri Aste welcomed Rene with warmth and love over and over and over again, you can welcome hurting kids with your own consistent, loving touch. Rene wasn't a perfect kid, and many of those coming into your home won't be either. They might not use good manners. They might break a vase or get mud on your couch. Their language might be a little rough. But you can offer them love and forgiveness anyway.

When Jesus said, "Let the little children come to me," he was welcoming them into his arms.[2] He didn't care if they whined, had runny noses, or put their dirty hands on his tunic. He just loved them.

Remember the old commercials for Kool-Aid drink mix? There was always one home in the neighborhood where all the kids hung out—and the commercial wanted us to believe it was because the mom served Kool-Aid. But while it's true that kids will always be attracted to fun food, that's not our best drawing card. Children enjoy coming to our homes most when we offer a consistent touch of the love and warmth of Jesus.

Geri Aste's love changed Rene's life forever. Are there children in your neighborhood, church, or extended family for whom you can do the same? You don't have to be a Kool-Aid mom. Just be an open-arms mom, offering touches of love that will forever change hurting young hearts.

Gracious Lord, help me to extend forgiveness, love, and a caring heart to rowdy children, sullen teens, and every other person who crosses my path.

Be kind and compassionate to one another,
forgiving each other, just as in Christ God forgave you.
—Ephesians 4:32

I want people to look at me and know I'm a Christian;
I am a child of God.
—Andrea Rozum, "I Am"

Andi's Poem

My friend Ann Marie is a teacher at a public high school. We all know how important a teacher's touch can be in the lives of her students, and Ann Marie could tell you many stories about teenagers she's been able to impact with kindness, grace, and love. But the story I want her to share with you is not about her own touch. It's about the touch of one of her students, Andrea—who also happens to be Ann Marie's daughter. Since Ann Marie has a beautiful way with words, I'll let her tell the story:

> My freshman English class was wrapping up a unit on poetry, and the final grade was based on individual portfolios of their cumulative work. On the last day of school we arranged our desks in a circle to give students "the floor" as each read three poems aloud from his or her portfolio.
>
> It's always fun to hear students read their creative work, and I think poetry is an excellent avenue for them to reveal their most sincere thoughts. That's why I was particularly disturbed to hear one young man's poems—each was, without exception, vile and confrontational. Many in the class snickered and hid smiles as he read one poem about his hatred for teachers and the violence he'd like to see come to them.
>
> The class looked at me expectantly when he finished. Protocol was to ask the other students for constructive comments following each reading, but this young man had offered me a clear challenge. I decided I would respond, but not in the classroom arena—that would come later with the school counselor.

Instead, I solicited input from the students. Many continued the joke, congratulating him on his creativity and descriptive language. This was especially disheartening because the April 20, 1999, Columbine High School tragedy was still fresh on all our minds, and I'd hoped they'd be especially sensitive to issues of violence.

The poetry readings continued, and finally it was Andrea's turn. I knew which poem she wanted to read aloud, but she had also confided in me that she didn't think she had the nerve. As I watched her shuffle through her papers, I held my breath. Finally, she drew one out...and then she began to read.

Because I know her, I detected the slight tremor in her voice that belied her composure. I'm sure that if anyone looked closely enough they'd have noticed her hands trembling slightly. But still she read with conviction and with the strength that comes from a sincere heart:

I am a child of God
I wonder what heaven will be like
I hear the angels' singing voices at the Rapture
I see innocent people getting killed because of their beliefs
I want people to look at me and know I'm a Christian
I am a child of God

I pretend in my mind that I'm a character of the Bible
I feel the presence of the devil
I touch the hand of God
I worry about my friends who don't know God
I cry when someone dies who doesn't know Christ
I am a child of God

I understand that Christ died to pay for my sins
I say there's no way to heaven except through Christ
I dream about the day I'll see God face to face
I try to be a good example for my non-Christian friends
I hope that I'll see my friends in heaven someday
I am a child of God[3]

When she finished, she stared silently at the paper in her hand. I think she was steeling herself for taunting and ridicule. The class followed her silence for a moment, and then a hand shot up. It was a quiet student who usually sat in the back of the room.

"I'm a Christian too. I think it took guts to read what Andi did. I always want to say stuff like that out loud, but for some reason I just don't. I'm glad she did."

Another hand, and "I really liked that poem. I'm a Christian, and I think it's good that she was brave enough to read her poem out loud."

And more: "I'm a Christian too!"

"Me too!"

"So am I!"

Andrea flushed with just a slight smile, but I know she was elated. I glanced at the student who'd read the "I hate teachers" poem and caught him exchanging bewildered looks with others in the room who usually laughed at his disruptions. They were clearly outnumbered—and the numbers seemed to be growing as more and more hands were lifted to affirm this poem about Christianity. A bond of common belief was forming.

Christ in the classroom! I can't legally teach about him, but I cannot stop a student from expressing herself if she wants to write about the God she loves. Since that day Andi has felt emboldened to not only live as an example for Christ, but to talk freely about her faith no matter the forum. Even on the volleyball court she has grown to be a leader, and I think one reason is that her leader is God.[4]

What an incredible testimony to the power a woman's touch can have! Ann Marie obviously touched the lives of her students over the school year, but even more, she touched the life of her daughter with the truth and love of God. And her daughter, in turn, found the courage to touch the lives of her classmates. Before Andrea read her poem, many of the teenagers had felt like outcasts in a society that glorifies hate, violence, sex, and every other kind of sin. They were afraid not only to take a strong stand for their beliefs but to even admit to others that they were Christians. Andrea's poem gave them the courage they needed—and took away the glory of one hateful boy who had tried to stir up hate in the hearts of others.

Have you ever felt ashamed of your faith? Have you ever been around people who ridiculed Christians? In America we don't experience the severe persecution that Christians in other countries do, but we are often the brunt of jokes and are discouraged from speaking openly about Jesus. The impact of the mockery and jeering adds up, and we become quieter and quieter about our love for Christ. Have you seen this in your own life?

In Matthew 5:14–16, Jesus says, "You are the light of the world. A city on a hill cannot be hidden. Neither do people light a lamp and put it under a bowl. Instead they put it on its stand, and it gives light to everyone in the house. In the same way, let your light shine before men, that they may see your good deeds and praise your Father in heaven." No matter how difficult it seems at the time, we must let our lights shine! It was difficult for Andrea to read her poem aloud in a room that seemed hostile. Yet this young woman reached out to leave an imprint of faith and love on those around her.

You can't touch the lives of others if you're hiding. Take a risk. Step out. You'll be surprised to find that other people are stepping out with you.

Powerful God, when the world tries to inject me and others with its hateful venom, give me the courage to touch people with your light and love instead.

Don't let anyone look down on you because you are young,
but set an example for the believers in speech, in life,
in love, in faith and in purity.
—1 Timothy 4:12

Sew, Sew

How do you think people will remember you when you die? What will they say at your memorial service? What do you think they'll chisel on your tombstone? Tom Sawyer got to find out. In the famous book by Mark Twain, Tom's family and friends thought he was dead. But he was very much alive and thoroughly enjoying himself as he eavesdropped on their weepy conversations about him!

The Bible tells us of a woman named Tabitha who really did die—and still got to find out how people remembered her. We don't have many details about her age or appearance or what caused her death. We simply know that she got sick and died. And according to the customs of that time, her body was washed and placed in a room in her home.

Tabitha was well known in her community as a woman of compassion and mercy. We read in Acts 9:36 that she "was always doing good and helping the poor." When the apostle Peter arrived at her home shortly after her death, many widows came up to him, crying because their dear friend was gone. Tabitha had been a seamstress, and during her lifetime she had often made clothing for them and for others in need. Now these widows gathered around Peter, showing him the robes and other articles Tabitha had once sewn for them out of the goodness of her heart. Can you hear them?

"Look at this warm dress Tabitha made for me—just in time for winter. She was so thoughtful."

"Tabitha really cared about people. See, here's a robe she made for my son when she saw him shivering in a doorway last year."

121

"She cared about how I looked when I hardly cared myself. This is the beautiful outfit she sewed for me when I was used to wearing only rags."

After listening for a while, Peter must have gotten a good picture of the kind of compassionate, giving woman Tabitha was. Sending the mourners from the room, he got down on his knees and prayed. Then he turned toward the woman's lifeless body and said, "Tabitha, get up." Immediately she opened her eyes and sat up. Peter helped her to her feet and presented her alive to her family and friends. Can you imagine the excitement—Tabitha had been raised from the dead!

Tabitha's miracle must have been the talk of the town for days, even weeks afterward. But what happened when all the commotion finally died down? The Bible doesn't tell us, but it's my guess that Tabitha went right back to doing the same things she'd been doing before—sewing clothes, doing good, and taking care of those in need.

There's a woman alive today who reminds me of Tabitha. No, she didn't get to disrupt her own funeral, but she has the same giving spirit. Her name is Karen Loucks-Baker. One Christmas Eve, Karen read an account of a little girl with cancer who made it through her treatments with the aid of her security blanket. The image of that child stuck in Karen's mind.

"I couldn't stop thinking about how many other sick children there must be who would love to have security blankets," she shares. So she decided to take action. She called a local newspaper and got the message out that she was collecting quilts for seriously ill children in local hospitals.

"I thought it would be great if I could collect a hundred blankets in six months," Karen remembers. "I had more than that in a few weeks!" The effort grew into what is now called Project Linus, after the blanket-carrying character from the *Peanuts* comic strip. There are now more than one hundred chapters of this organization around the country, with thousands of quilts being put into the hands of sick children who must spend lonely nights in hospital wards.[5]

Tabitha had the ability to sew, and she put her talents to good use serving those in her community. Karen Loucks-Baker has a compassionate heart and the aptitude for organization. She put her abilities to use first in her own community and then throughout the entire United

States. What these women saw as small contributions toward a better world meant the world to those whose lives they touched.

What touch do you have on your community? There are so many ways to get involved! Organizations large and small are in desperate need of volunteers—in nursing homes and soup kitchens, in crisis pregnancy centers and homeless shelters. People are needed to deliver meals and medicine to those who can't leave their homes. Tutors are needed for disadvantaged schoolchildren. The list could go on and on!

What talents or abilities can you offer? Can you send a quilt to Karen and the children touched through Project Linus? Can you sort canned goods at a food bank? Can you drive a blind woman to a doctor's appointment? Of course you can. The real question is, will you?

When the time comes for your memorial service, I hope the church is packed with people who can attest to your love for them and for Jesus because of the way you touched their lives. If you haven't reached out to your community before now, get started. Maybe you won't have to wait until your funeral to know that your touch is needed and appreciated.

Compassionate Father, you wrap me in the security blanket of your love. Show me the best ways I can touch my community and help bring others into this warm embrace.

Blessed are those who mourn,
for they will be comforted.
—Matthew 5:4

Lord, if you can't make me thin, make my friends look fat.
—Erma Bombeck in *Making Life Rich Without Any Money*

You Go, Girl!

Many of my friends have e-mail, and they often find great little quotes, stories, and other tidbits to forward my way. One of the items that popped up on my computer screen one morning was the following list—"The Top Ten Things Only Women Understand." As a woman, you'll appreciate it!

10. Cats' facial expressions

9. The need for the same style of shoes in different colors

8. Why bean sprouts aren't just weeds

7. Fat clothes

6. Taking a car trip without trying to beat your best time

5. The difference between beige, off-white, and eggshell

4. Cutting your bangs to make them grow

3. Eyelash curlers

2. The inaccuracy of every bathroom scale ever made

And here's the number one thing only women understand:

1. Other women[6]

Although I don't get number ten—I personally have no idea what cats are thinking—I do agree that no one seems to understand me like my girlfriends. My husband can't comprehend how I can go for a long walk around the lake with my sister, have lunch with her in the afternoon, and still have some reason to talk to her on the phone an hour later. (You understand perfectly, don't you?)

Men in general don't seem to get the concept of eating half a salad for lunch so you can have chocolate cheesecake for dessert. They're confused about why we go to the rest room in groups. They see positively no point in acquiring a taste for Diet Coke. Certain things, I'm convinced, can only be understood by the female sex.

Some women tell me they have lots of guys for friends and don't really relate to other women. I don't buy that for a minute. You've got to have girlfriends. Sometimes a man just won't do.

Let me give you an example. During a summer between college semesters, I went shopping for my wedding dress. My roommates had gone home for the break, however, so I decided to take one of my guy friends along to help me make my choice. Did he "ooh" and "aah" over the fabric, running the various materials through his fingers to get an idea of how it would lay? Did he laugh at some of the dorky bridesmaid dresses on display, or catch on that "You'll be able to wear this again!" is a standard lie brides tell their friends? Did he insist that I try on a certain dress because he'd seen it modeled in *Bride* magazine? Of course not!

Instead, he shifted his feet awkwardly, pretended he wasn't there, and barely hid his excitement when I told him I didn't need his help anymore because I'd decided to make the gown myself. I realized then that in some situations, a woman's touch is a must!

Today my girlfriends are a big part of my life. My friend Lori understands the finer points of canning, is willing to stand on a stage and do goofy motions to songs while singing with kids, and cried with me when we found out our adoption had fallen through. My friend Sheila always makes sure friends who are sick are prayed for and have meals delivered. She and Lori were the ones who helped gather a crowd to paint our home when my husband went through months of chronic illness.

My friend Tricia has a wildly creative ability to change a drab bedroom into a little girl's fantasy—while abiding by a strict budget. She also has a tender heart, always tucking away neat little items she finds here and there to give later to a person in need. She's the queen of hospitality—and besides that, she has never disclosed to my anticoffee husband how much caffeine I actually drink when I'm sitting in her kitchen.

My friend Nancy can make delicious desserts with secret ingredients like baby food. She sneaks chocolate onto my doorstep. (I figured out it was you, sweetie—but don't stop!) She, too, is a writer, and we often talk shop about our shared profession. I could go on and on telling you about other friends—each one holding a special place in my heart. No matter how thoughtful and sensitive a man can be, he can never be a substitute for a great girlfriend.

Think about your own friends. Each one has qualities that make her special and different from the others. One might be a great listener with a shoulder that's perfect for you to cry on. Another might share a hobby or interest with you. Another might have a wacky sense of humor that cheers you up no matter what. Each friend touches your life in a different way. Each friend adds a unique scent to the perfume of your life.

Proverbs 27:9 reminds us of two things. The first is that the aroma of a beautiful perfume (I like to think of the smell of something chocolate baking in the oven!) can bring joy to your heart. The second is that good advice from a friend can be just as sweet. In other words, the counsel and encouragement of a dear friend can bring you as much joy as a bouquet of roses or a pan of warm brownies. And who doesn't need a good, chewy brownie now and then?

A listening ear, helpful hands, arms that wrap around you—these are gifts from God designed to lift your spirits and bring you much needed moments of refreshment and delight. Do you appreciate these gifts? Have you ever thought of thanking your friends for their touch in your life? In her book *Thanks for Being My Friend*, Judy Harper Spaar lists hundreds of reasons for thanking these special people. You might want to call a friend today and say something like:

- Thanks for telling me how my new dress really looked.

- Thanks for getting my prescription filled when I was too sick to drive.

- Thanks for ironing my skirt when I was late for my job interview.

- Thanks for worrying about me.

- Thanks for waiting to make sure my car starts before driving away.

❧ Thanks for taking a picture of a rainbow and sending it to me.[7]

Take time to make your own list of reasons to say thank you. Then take a friend some flowers or leave chocolate in her mailbox or show up at her back door with lattes to share. Be sure your friend knows how much you appreciate her touch. And use your thank-you list to spark ideas for touching her life in return.

That raises the question: What kind of friend are you? Are you the sensitive friend who knows when others are up or down? The loyal, "call-me-anytime-day-or-night" friend? The thoughtful friend who tucks treats in pockets or sends notes of encouragement? Do you pray for your friends? Do you share with them the joy of knowing Jesus?

What is it about you that makes other women want to have you as a friend? What is it about your touch that keeps them coming back for more? Or is there something in your manner that drives potential friends away—things like gossip, a persistently negative attitude, rudeness, anger, or self-absorption? You might not think about it much, but you are impacting the lives of your friends by your attitude toward them and your treatment of them. You are leaving a permanent fingerprint on them—just as they are on you.

Don't let that mark be one of disappointment or pain. Friends don't give friends scars! Instead, friends touch the lives of others with a beautiful aroma that lingers long after they're gone. Determine today to show your friends the kind of love, acceptance, and appreciation that will be a blessing in their lives for years to come.

Lord, thank you for friends—they're the sunshine that makes our hearts grow. Help me to appreciate the touch my friends have on my life, and teach me to be a better friend in return.

Perfume and incense bring joy to the heart,
and the pleasantness of one's friend springs from his earnest counsel.
—Proverbs 27:9

Success is 99 percent perspiration…
and 1 percent avoidance of the bubonic plague.
—Xena in *Life Lessons from Xena the Warrior Princess:*
A Guide to Happiness, Success, and Body Armor

Rules of Thumb

"Our vision: To be a body of believers who are daily touching 'our world' with the love and power of Jesus Christ."

I hear this phrase and quote it in unison with other folks at least once a month. It's the vision statement of the church I belong to, and our pastor likes to keep it fresh in our minds—a regular reminder of what "church" is all about. I particularly like the "our world" part. As Christians, we don't have to feel overwhelmed about touching the whole world for Jesus. We just have to be faithful in touching our world—the people God has set within our own sphere of influence.

As we continue to think about the significance of a woman's touch, let's take some time to think about our personal spheres of influence. What are the smaller communities we're touching regularly? These might include:

- people we know through our children, such as other parents, soccer moms, and teachers
- our friends
- people at church
- neighbors and their kids
- acquaintances from clubs, discussion groups, even on-line chat rooms
- our family members, both immediate and extended
- classmates at school

❧ those we encounter at places where we volunteer

❧ coworkers, clients, and other business associates

We've considered how our touch impacts many of these people in other sections of this book. But one group we've not discussed much is the last one: coworkers and business associates. The Bible says we're supposed to be "Christ's ambassadors, as though God were making his appeal through us."[8] Nowhere is this more important than in the workplace. Even if you work in a "Christian" organization, you are certain to encounter people who don't share your beliefs in Christ and who need God's love in their lives. How are you going to touch them for Jesus?

The best way is to do the obvious: your job! Even better, go above and beyond the call of duty. When I worked in the area of human resources, I was amazed at how many people complained about losing their jobs or not getting raises yet admitted they weren't doing their work. One girl in my department regularly came to work drunk or so tired that she repeatedly fell asleep at her desk. She wasn't trying to touch the world for Jesus, but she certainly touched everyone in the office by making our jobs more difficult.

By doing your job efficiently and effectively, you touch those around you in a positive way and make their lives better. Be on time to work. Don't leave early. Follow company procedures. Turn in projects on time. Of course, sometimes things happen that are beyond your control, and mistakes occur. But doing your best reflects positively on you as a Christian woman and on the God you serve.

Second, show integrity. Be honest. Follow through. Don't promise what you can't deliver. If you're an attorney, don't use loopholes in the law to get around a fair verdict. If you sell cars, tell the truth about what's under the hood. If you're an accountant, don't make the numbers lie to improve the bottom line. If you're an office worker, keep an honest record of your hours—including your time off for lunch. Jesus said, "I am the way and the *truth* and the life."[9] You honor Christ when you are honest and aboveboard in all your words and actions.

Third, steer clear of gossip. James called the tongue "a fire…a restless evil, full of deadly poison."[10] The power of a loose tongue can destroy both the person being talked about and the person doing the talking. Not only do you ruin the reputation of another by spreading rumors, stories, and other information that's none of your business, you damage your reputation and the reputation of Christ. People will know they can't confide in you—unless they want the whole world to know about their struggles.

Fourth, guard your reputation. So many women in the workplace don't think about this one! You may genuinely care about the troubles of the man in the next office and strive to touch him with the love of Jesus through your caring words, encouraging notes, and quick hugs. Be careful! Not only are you leaving yourself open to being swayed by your own emotions, you might be sending the wrong messages to this man. And you're under the scrutiny of coworkers who will certainly begin to wonder about your relationship. Make every effort to avoid even the appearance of impropriety. There are ways to touch others with God's love without overstepping the bounds of godly character.

Last of all, listen. This is how you'll know the hurts your coworkers are enduring. If you're always the one doing the talking, others won't have a chance to open up—and you can't touch them if you don't know their needs. Being quick to listen and slow to speak isn't just my advice, it comes straight from the Bible.[11]

Understand, I'm not offering these suggestions from an ivory tower. I've been in the working world. I once had a job where I got sucked into the gossip mill, and I'm sad to say the touch I ended up leaving on that office was one of bitterness rather than joy. Later I had a job where I tried hard to avoid gossip and to listen instead to the hearts of the people around me; one of my coworkers became a Christian as a result. And while I've never compromised my reputation, I've seen Christian men and women fall into the temptation of sex in the workplace—and I've cried over the resulting devastation in their homes, their businesses, and the Christian community as a whole.

Even if you're not in the workplace, these guidelines can still apply—in friendships, in volunteer situations, in clubs, in neighborhoods. As an ambassador for Christ, you point others to him whenever your life exemplifies the principles of excellence, integrity, self-control, purity, and compassion. These are characteristics that are in short supply in *every* arena of life.

One last word of advice: As you try to live a life that honors God, don't cop a "holier-than-thou" attitude. That's a surefire way to turn people away from you and away from Jesus. Don't worry about how others are living. Instead, simply apply the basic principles of Christ to your own life. People in every corner of "your world" are certain to be touched.

Lord, help me to touch others daily with your love and power—whether I'm at work or play.

He who pursues righteousness and love finds life,
prosperity and honor.
—Proverbs 21:21

THE HANDS OF GOD

Touching in and through Your Church

God has given us two hands—one to receive with and the other to give with. We are not cisterns made for hoarding; we are channels made for giving.
—Billy Graham in *Friends*

First Contact

How did you find your church? Did you visit on the recommendation of a friend? Did you try the one closest to your home? Did you simply look up the denomination of your choice in the Yellow Pages and begin visiting?

Finding the right church for you and your family can be a long and trying process. There's so much to consider: the quality of the children's programs, the style of music, the practicality of the preacher's messages, even the drive time. Yet when I polled members of my own church and asked why they chose to attend there, the comment I heard over and over was, "The people are friendly." Sure, some people remarked about the singing, the preaching, the classes, and the nursery. But the friendliness of the congregation was the number one factor, hands-down.

I realize my research wasn't scientific, but I do believe the touch of friendliness in a church brings people back for more. That's certainly been the case in my own life.

When our son was just three months old, Mike and I moved to Phoenix. We visited three or four churches in our community and enjoyed different aspects of each one. We probably could have joined any of these churches, become involved, and felt a part of the ministry there. But at the time it seemed that none of them "clicked" with us— we couldn't put our finger on exactly why.

Then one Sunday we tried yet another church. We walked up to the information booth and asked, "Where's the nursery?"

Instead of handing us a map or pointing down a corridor, one of the women answered, "I'll take you there." She walked beside us, told us her name was Tish, and offered her assistance if we had any other questions. Before we knew it, we were at the door of the nursery, handing Tony to a smiling nursery worker. We exchanged a few more pleasantries, then Tish headed back to the information booth, and we made our way to the sanctuary.

After the service, we returned to the nursery to retrieve Tony. Tish was there too. "Hey, I just wanted to let you know about a Bible study my husband and I have in our home," she began. We listened, said we'd think about joining the study, and went home. A few days later the phone rang, and it was Tish. "I know you're new to the area, and a few other moms and I are getting together with our kids for a picnic today. Want to come?"

I did want to go, but we only had one car, and Mike had driven it to work.

"No problem," Tish said. "Tell me where you live, and I'll come get you."

I had a great time with the other mothers, and I enjoyed getting to know Tish a little better as we drove around town that day. The next Sunday, Tish brought her husband to meet us at the nursery. They invited us to join them and three other couples at their home for lunch after church. We said yes—and our church search was over. We joined Tish and Seldon's Bible study group, we joined the church, and we even got involved with leading the college group. We'd found our church home.

Years later, we said a tearful good-bye to our friends in Phoenix and moved to Colorado. The church search was on again! It was wintertime, and my husband decided to go to the local Wal-Mart to do some Christmas shopping. As he left the store, he saw a group of women sitting at a table, wrapping presents. Their sign mentioned the name of a local church and clearly stated that their gift-wrapping service was free of charge.

"Free gift wrap?" one of them asked brightly.

Not being too handy with paper and tape, Mike was only too glad to hand over his purchases. Then he stood back and watched.

"Surely they're going to slip gospel tracts into the boxes," he thought. They didn't. "I'll bet they're going to want me to listen to a short presentation about their church," he mused. They didn't.

"Certainly they'll ask for a donation," he reflected. Wrong again. Mike watched the women cheerfully wrap his gifts and the gifts of many others who wandered out of the store. One man had a huge box, a Ping-Pong table. "You wouldn't take one this big..." he said, politely declining their offer. "Sure we would!" they replied with a smile, and began measuring.

"I want to try their church," Mike said when he came home that day. "The people were so friendly, so cheery, and they didn't expect anything in return." So the next Sunday we drove to their building and found out that the gift-wrapping women were just a few of many friendly people in that congregation. We've been going there ever since. We've even joined the gift-wrapping crew on many chilly December mornings, reaching out to touch others in the same way we were touched.

People everywhere, it seems, have the same need to feel valuable, wanted, and loved. And that should be right up our alley! Jesus said Christians should be known by their love—not by their T-shirts or bumper stickers, their huge church buildings or snazzy bands, their fiery preaching or clean nurseries. They should be known *by their love*. As Christians and as churches, we should be touching our communities with the kind of love that says: You are valuable. You are wanted. God loves you so much!

Unfortunately, we often forget this simple truth and act more condemning than loving toward others. That leaves a "love vacuum" in many searching souls—an emptiness that hundreds of secular groups and cults are only too eager to fill. Many of these groups set up shop near college campuses, shopping malls, or other places where they know they'll find people looking for love and acceptance—easy prey, so to speak.

In college, I knew a Christian girl who decided to write a research paper on a particular cult. To augment her research, she visited a meeting of the local chapter. She was so overwhelmed by the love and acceptance these people showered on her that she converted to their beliefs within weeks. What a powerful touch love is!

Think about this: When you invite people into your home, how do you treat them? Do you shake hands, show them where to sit, then leave to watch television or read a book? Do you talk only to your husband and ignore your guests? Do you pick up the phone and start chatting with someone else? Of course not! You do everything you can to make your guests feel comfortable and welcome in your home.

It should be the same way in our churches. Our church is like our home. We already know our way around, we already know the routines, and we already know the people who "live" there. Yet it's fairly common for us to drop off our kids at Sunday school, find our favorite pew, and talk only to our good friends—ignoring anyone we aren't sure we've seen before.

Is this you? Are you making the guests at your church feel welcomed and loved? Are you giving them a reason to come back? I know that the women who reached out to Mike and me were the catalysts in our decisions to join their churches. When we knew someone cared, we wanted to belong. Will you show new people in your church that you care?

Many women have gone to great lengths to leave their mark upon the world. We've talked about some of them in this book. You might think, "I could never do what she did." *This* is something you can do. Welcome someone at church this week. Invite that person to dinner. Call him or her during the week to be sure any questions were adequately answered. Follow up.

Offer the love that Jesus said you'd be known for. Offer your touch.

Lord, you have welcomed me into your heart with great joy. Now
help me to step out of my comfort zone and welcome others who are
in need of your love.

By this all men will know that you are my disciples,
if you love one another.
—John 13:35

Reach anew to God, then reach to each other.
Only then can you reach out to the world.
—Anne Ortlund in *The Christian Daily Planner 2000*

Church Ladies

On a recent Sunday, a lady at our church stood up and encouraged the women of the congregation to join her in a ministry to a nearby shelter for battered women.

"The women at the shelter are at their lowest point," she explained. "They've been hurt by those they thought loved them. They need to know *God* loves them. We can give them gift baskets to let them know God's love through our touch."

She held up a huge basket filled with items like scented lotions and bath oils, aromatic candles, chocolates, flavored teas and coffees, and other goodies that would make any woman feel spoiled. "If you'll bring some of these items to our next meeting," she said, "we can put the baskets together and take them to the shelter." What a great idea—and what a blessing those baskets were to the women who received them!

As we consider the various ways we can touch people through our churches, I thought you might be encouraged to know what women in churches around the country are doing to touch the world with God's love. Of course, many churches offer women's Bible studies or preschool and day-care services. These are wonderful touches, but I want to share some ideas you might not have considered. Maybe one will spark a flame in your heart to do the same.

Prison outreach. A group of women from several churches in my area makes regular visits to women at a nearby prison who are hurting and in desperate need of love and teaching. The church group leads a time of singing and Bible study, then they pray with the women for their various needs and concerns. The group is also sensitive to

138

the children hurt by their mothers' crimes; each Christmas, they gather small items for the imprisoned women to give as presents to their kids.[1]

Study hall. With so many "latch-key" children left at home after school while their parents are working, one group of women thought it would be a good idea to open up a room at their church as a place for schoolchildren to come for a snack and study hall. This isn't a place where kids come to play and goof off. Instead, they're offered a nutritious snack and directed to tables where they can read and do their homework. The women try to help the kids with their work and tutor them if they're able.

Food and clothing bank. This project calls for women with good organization skills. One closet or small room in the church facility is designated for storing nonperishable food items and clean clothing (in good condition!) donated by church members. The items are then given away to those in need, using whatever method of distribution the church agrees upon. (By letting local service agencies know about the food and clothing bank, a steady stream of people are certain to come for help.) In one variation to this idea, a group of women I know holds an annual "clothing exchange." They collect used clothing for both children and adults, sort it into sizes, and invite people to come on the exchange day to pick up items for free.

Oil change and minor car repair service. Most women prefer to leave mechanical stuff to the guys, but even I can change the oil in a car. I've heard of churches gathering a few "handy" women and offering to change the oil and do other simple car repairs once a month for single mothers in the community. Sometimes a local auto supply store will even donate the oil.

Services clearinghouse. One group of women got all the ladies at their church to fill out a survey listing services they'd be willing to do now and then at no charge. Now when someone in the church or community has a need, the group matches the need with one of these willing servants. The group has coordinated meals for people in times of crisis or illness, rides for the vision-impaired, help with minor home repairs and yard work, mending for nursing home residents, and much more.

Mentoring program. The women in this ministry take Titus 2:4 to heart: "Then [the older women] can train the younger women…" More mature Christians are paired with younger women (both teens and women in their early twenties) who are looking for a friend and a little guidance. Some of the younger women are unwed mothers, some are looking for college or career direction, some need help with housekeeping skills. The two women meet regularly each week or each month for a time of sharing, counsel, and prayer.

Baby showers for women with crisis pregnancies. Many Christians are willing to protest abortion yet quick to shun unwed mothers. Some women have tried to go against this flow by teaming with their local crisis pregnancy center to throw baby showers on a regular basis. All the gifts go to help women in crisis pregnancies who've made the brave decision to carry their babies to term. The children of these women—often born into less-than-ideal circumstances—need diapers, bottles, clothing, books, and toys just as much (if not more) than babies with married parents. Both mothers and children are shown God's love through this kind of ministry.

As you can imagine, I could go on and on. Christian women are very creative when it comes to finding ways to touch the world around them! The touches I've mentioned here—along with so many others—not only impact people in our churches, they reach into the community and bring those who don't know Jesus one step closer to meeting him.

Jesus was clear in Matthew 25:35–36 that when we minister to the needs of others, we're really ministering to him. When we provide food for a hungry family, show kindness toward a hurting individual, donate baby clothes to an unwed mother, pray with a sick person in the hospital, or take a Bible to a prisoner, we do these things as unto the Lord. And surely none of us would knowingly turn Jesus away!

Look around your community. There are so many people in need! Do you see them? What do you see when you look in their eyes? Begin today to see Jesus! Then join together with other women and do what you can to help. Together you can touch your congregation, your community, and your world with the love of God.

Father, thank you for all the ways you've provided for me. Help me to be willing to go the extra mile to provide for others. Remind me again and again that when I serve others, I serve you.

For I was hungry and you gave me something to eat,
I was thirsty and you gave me something to drink,
I was a stranger and you invited me in,
I needed clothes and you clothed me,
I was sick and you looked after me,
I was in prison and you came to visit me.
—Matthew 25:35–36

Well, today's eight-year-olds are tomorrow's teenagers.
I say this calls for action and now! Nip it in the bud!
First sign of youngsters going wrong, you've got to nip it in the bud.
—Barney Fife in *The Andy Griffith Show*

Young Hearts

It seems you can't turn on the news or read the newspaper today without hearing about teenagers who are in trouble: young women giving birth and leaving their babies in trash cans, teens driving drunk and killing others in car wrecks, high schoolers building bombs or shooting their classmates. And every time these tragedies come up in discussion around the dinner table, by the water cooler, in on-line chat rooms, or in the media, everyone asks the same thing: "Why didn't somebody stop them? Why doesn't somebody do something?"

But kids don't come up to strangers and say, "Hey, I think I'm going to get into trouble today. Want to try and talk me out of it?" They don't invite your input or mine. Before they get involved in destructive activities, they're often seen hanging around the local movie theaters, malls, or bowling alleys, trying to look cool or threatening or a little of both. When you see them you probably clutch your purse a little closer, avoid eye contact, and speed up your pace until you're safely past. Or maybe you give them a glare of annoyance that says, "Don't you know any better? Don't you have something constructive to do?" The teenagers who are headed for actions of tragic consequence usually aren't the kind you walk up to and invite home for tea!

I could very well have been one of those teens headed for trouble. Maybe you could have been too. Sure, I had my good side. I was an honor student involved in student government. I won awards for my leadership skills. I never missed church. I held a job. And being the oldest of five kids, I was the responsible big sister. Most people thought I was on my way up in the world.

But there were times I knew I was on my way down. I was a

preacher's kid, and true to the stereotype that goes with children of ministers, I had a rebellious streak. I didn't want to be the perfect kid who always knew the answers in Sunday school!

So while most of my friends were the "good," upstanding teens in the community, I also had a few friends who saw nothing wrong with leading me along a wayward path. I *knew* the difference between right and wrong, but I also wanted to be loved and accepted by people other than my parents. If the "bad" crowd would love me for who I was (and not for who my father was), then they were the ones I wanted to hang out with.

Fortunately, several factors kept me from rushing headlong toward disaster. For one, people were praying for me. Second, I had a firm enough foundation to make the right decisions more often than not. And third, God's grace was at work. But there was a fourth factor that was at least as important as the other three: Several women took me under their wing and loved me, pimples and all.

Beccy, Carol, and Patty were single career women I knew from church. They'd finished college and were well into their successful lives in retail, medicine, and music. They certainly had no need for a flirtatious and giggly teenager. But for some reason these women decided to involve me in their lives.

Beccy invited me to go on several weekend trips with her. We always shopped and ate and had fun, but mostly we talked. Carol made lunch for me once a week and asked questions about the choices I was making, the friendships I was developing, and the direction my life was taking. She had a silly side and loved to involve me in her pranks or various projects. Patty let me talk her ear off on cross-country ski trips, asking for more details even when she must have been tired of hearing my silly teenage opinions. Together with other singles from the church we played cards and board games, rented mountain cabins, prayed, threw snowballs, read the Bible, and stayed up late.

I still have no idea what compelled these women to befriend me— but I'm eternally grateful. During those hours we spent together, something of each one of them rubbed off on me. Their touch stayed with me. I think especially of Beccy and the long hours we spent in her blue Maverick (which I later bought). She opened her heart and shared with me mistakes she'd made in her life and how God's grace had brought her through those times. I kept her words in my heart for years, and when I found myself making the same mistakes I knew I could follow Beccy's example. I could ask God's forgiveness, turn my life around, and start afresh. And I did.

Now there's a young teenager from our church in my life. She reminds me so much of myself at that age. She's had a great upbringing with strong Christian parents and the best in education. But she's floundering. She's hanging out with the wrong people, making poor choices regarding school and career. She's trying to stand with her feet in two worlds, putting off the inevitability of having to commit to one or the other.

I have no idea why this girl likes to hang out with me. All I seem to do is agree with her parents and warn her of the trouble that's ahead if she chooses the wrong course. But she keeps coming back for more. We keep having lunch together, and I keep asking her questions about the choices she's making, the friendships she's developing, and the direction her life is taking. I try to be honest. I try to let her know I care. I don't know what the years will bring or what difference my touch will make in her life. All I know is that many years ago someone took the time to touch my life, and it made a difference. Surely I can do the same.

Remember those teenagers we were talking about earlier, the ones who were just hanging around, waiting for trouble? Every one of them needs a friend. Every one of them needs Jesus. And every one of them is headed down a path of destruction unless someone stops them.

Stop them with your love—not all of them, perhaps, but at least one. Find a teenage girl in your church and invite her over for lunch or out for ice cream. Even if she seems to have her life together, I guarantee she has a million questions and plenty of needs. Go shopping together or help her make cookies for her boyfriend. Let her know you count her as a friend. Tell her you honestly care.

It's this kind of touch that makes a difference in the life of a teenager—and that lets her know God's love for her is real. It tells her that he really does care about the choices she's making, the friendships she's developing, and the direction her life is taking. "For I know the plans I have for you," God says in Jeremiah 29:11, "plans to prosper you and not to harm you, plans to give you hope and a future." What a wonderful promise to share with a teenager! Won't you open your heart today, and let God love a teen through you?

Lord, give an extra measure of blessing to those women who reached out and touched me even when I wasn't really lovable. And let me follow their example!

I guide you in the way of wisdom
and lead you along straight paths.
When you walk, your steps will not be hampered;
when you run, you will not stumble.
—Proverbs 4:11–12

Dear God, Do you and Mr. Rogers talk to each other?
He is very wise.
—Anthony, age six, in *Dear God*

Kids' Church

I hate to admit this. In fact, I'm embarrassed to admit this. It might even come as a shock to some of you—so maybe you'd better sit down! Ready? *I don't remember any of my Sunday school lessons.*

It's true. I was raised in a Christian home and went to church every Sunday, even when we were on vacation. I must have learned something, because I can still sing the words to a zillion hymns and choruses, I know all the Bible stories, I can say the books of the Bible in order, and I have memorized many, many scripture verses. I clearly remember snack times—especially the part with the chocolate milk. And I remember the time our large family forgot one of my sisters and had to go back to church to get her once we realized she wasn't at home with us. But I cannot say that I remember one specific lesson or meaningful message spoken by my teachers.

What I do remember, however, are my teachers.

Ava was my Sunday school teacher when I was a preschooler. I don't remember her from those days and only know this information is true because my parents have told me. I have one picture of me at toddler age standing next to Ava, but the photo doesn't jog my memory. When I was three my family moved away, and Ava easily could have floated out of my life. Instead, she kept in touch with my family over the years. We visited her when we were back in that part of the country. She sent me a beautiful handmade cross-stitch picture when I graduated from high school. Just a couple of years ago, when I was filming a television appearance in her state, I looked out and saw her smiling face in the front row of the studio audience. We e-mail each other even today.

Over the years, I've heard Ava's charming southern accent, listened to her sing in front of her church, seen her face beam as she talks about her husband, and watched her raise her sons as a godly mother. I've grown to know and love Ava's mix of love, hospitality, and cheer. While I don't remember the words she spoke as my teacher, I remember the love she's shown me from the time I was two to the present day.

Linda was my Sunday school teacher when I was in the sixth grade. She was a pretty college student, and my friends and I really admired her. That year she took us under her wing. Our church, like many others, was strapped for space, and our group of about eight kids met in the tiny room where people changed their clothes before being baptized. (Obviously we were done with class before the baptisms began!) Linda let us decorate that closet of a room with posters to make it "our" space. She promised us at the beginning of the year that if we came to Sunday school each week, always brought our Bibles, and learned a certain number of scripture verses, she'd take us to Disneyland the following summer. You can be sure I met every requirement! And, faithful to her word, Linda took three of us to the Magic Kingdom that year. Linda made me feel special, and for a long time I wanted to be just like her. We've lost contact over the years, but I still remember her touch on my life.

Now I work in the children's ministry at my church, teaching kids week after week. Along with a team of leaders, I agonize over the best way to make a certain point, and I search for the most creative means to bringing children closer to Christ. For all my efforts, this is what kids tell me they remember:

- "I remember the time Jody accidentally set the carpet on fire." (That would be my sister Jody, who is also involved in children's ministry. She was doing a flaming object lesson that got a bit out of hand. The fire lasted five seconds, and the kids remember it two years later.)

- "I remember the week you were sick and we got to watch a *VeggieTales* video instead of doing our lesson."

- "I remember the time we gave money to the missionaries for blankets."

147

Chapter Eight: The Hands of God

❧"I remember the day we got to use glitter and glued it all over the table, and it was there for the rest of the year."

You see? They don't remember my great lesson on peer pressure or my creative teaching on Bible heroes. Does that mean all my efforts are in vain? Hardly! Even though the kids aren't able to articulate it, I am 100 percent sure they know I love God and I love them. I actually feel a bit like a celebrity in town when they see me at the store or post office or somewhere else. The girls run up to me, give me hugs, and chatter away about what they're doing. The boys saunter by and grin sheepishly as they coolly say hello. I ask them about school, the sports they're in, and the scoop on who got what parts in the school play. I tell them I'm praying for them—and I really am.

I've been in youth and children's ministry now for many years, and I've had a chance to see kids I've taught graduate from high school and college, begin careers, get married, even leave for the mission field. When they're back in town, they stop by to sit in my kitchen and drink hot chocolate. A couple of them visited recently and reminisced about the years they'd been a part of my group. One remembered how she had often opened her heart to me while we made cookies or pizza in my kitchen, and how I'd listened. Another said, "I am co-leading a small high school group, and every meeting makes me fondly remember our times at your house. I hope our kids receive as much from the group as we did back then."

I know these kids-turned-young-adults don't remember my exact words or specific lessons from their youth group days. But from the evidence of positive change and maturity in their lives, I know the message of God's love hit home, and they've applied what they learned.

Churches today are in dire need of women of all ages to take children into their hearts and touch them for eternity. Whether you can change diapers and wipe runny noses or host slumber parties and chaperone skate nights, these kids need to see you live out your relationship with Christ before them so they can follow your model. Long after the Sunday school lesson is over and the take-home pages are turned into paper airplanes, they'll remember you—not so much what you said, but how you lived, how you loved God, and how you loved them.

How can you get involved? What notices have been running in your church bulletin week after week? Do they need drivers for a road trip? A home where an after-school club can meet? A lap for rocking babies? Willing hands to prepare a snack or organize a craft session? Someone to sing with preschoolers?

The doors are open for you to share the love of Jesus with kids at your church. Please don't say, "I don't do children's ministry" or, "Someone younger should be involved with the youth." Jesus could have turned up his nose at the thought of washing the feet of his disciples, but it was his example of humility and love that left a permanent impression on those men and that touches us even today.

Make an impression. Let your touch be felt. There's blessing in it for the children—and for you!

Gracious Father, thank you for the children who are eager to know you more. Thank you for their energetic spirits and their open hearts. Please show me the way I can help to touch their hearts for you—without setting the carpet on fire.

Now that I, your Lord and Teacher, have washed your feet,
you also should wash one another's feet.
I have set you an example that you should do as I have done for you.
I tell you the truth, no servant is greater than his master,
nor is a messenger greater than the one who sent him.
Now that you know these things,
you will be blessed if you do them.
—John 13:14–17

We are all pencils in the hand of a writing God,
who is sending love letters to the world.
Mother Teresa in *The Christian Daily Planner 2000*

Support Your Local Pastor

Wanted: Applicant with college and graduate degrees (married man preferred). Must be an excellent public speaker and experienced counselor. Regular workweek demands a minimum of sixty hours, plus on-call status twenty-four hours a day. Must have the wisdom of Solomon and the patience of Job, capable of keeping many different kinds of people happy at all times. Lawn-mowing and plumbing skills a plus. Wife will be expected to volunteer on numerous committees. Children will be looked upon as a reflection of the applicant and should be silent, cheerful, and well behaved. Salary, very low. Benefits, next to none.

Who in the world would want such a job? Try your local pastor! Church pastors and ministry leaders are among the hardest worked and lowest paid of all employment groups. They must be at the church every time the doors are open, know everyone's name, keep a handle on the church budget, visit people in hospitals, do weddings and funerals, preach weekly sermons that stir everyone's hearts, be a spiritual leader to people who have diverse ideas and expectations of the pastor's role, and still have a smile on their faces at all times!

When my husband, Mike, worked in youth ministry, he interviewed with a number of churches. Most told him that their pastors were expected to work sixty to eighty hours a week to keep up with the demands of the congregation. When Mike asked how these pastors found time for their families, most just shrugged. One pastor said that he was able to spend time with his wife and kids each day—but only because he got up at 3 A.M. each day to get a jump on his work.

"Yes, I agree pastoring is a difficult job," you're probably saying. "But what has that got to do with me?"

To answer that question, let's look at the example of some women in the Bible. Luke 8:1–3 says, "After this, Jesus traveled about from one town and village to another, proclaiming the good news of the kingdom of God. The Twelve were with him, and also some women who had been cured of evil spirits and diseases: Mary (called Magdalene) from whom seven demons had come out; Joanna the wife of Cuza, the manager of Herod's household; Susanna; and many others. These women were helping to support them out of their own means."

Acts 16:13–15 tells us, "On the Sabbath we went outside the city gate to the river, where we expected to find a place of prayer. We sat down and began to speak to the women who had gathered there. One of those listening was a woman named Lydia, a dealer in purple cloth from the city of Thyatira, who was a worshiper of God. The Lord opened her heart to respond to Paul's message. When she and the members of her household were baptized, she invited us to her home. 'If you consider me a believer in the Lord,' she said, 'come and stay at my house.' And she persuaded us."

Now look at Acts 18:1–3: "After this, Paul left Athens and went to Corinth. There he met a Jew named Aquila, a native of Pontus, who had recently come from Italy with his wife Priscilla, because Claudius had ordered all the Jews to leave Rome. Paul went to see them, and because he was a tentmaker as they were, he stayed and worked with them."

We can read about some of the women mentioned in these verses elsewhere in the Bible. For others, this is the only time their names appear. But whether we know much about them or not, we can learn something from each one of them. Mary, Joanna, Susanna, Lydia, Priscilla—these women gave what they had, whether it was money, food, or lodging, to support Christ and his work. Just because Jesus, Paul, and their coworkers were preaching the gospel and doing great miracles doesn't mean they got a free ticket anywhere. They still had to pay for food and a roof over their heads. They still needed comfortable places to rest and recoup. The support of these women was indispensable.

My favorite is Lydia. I love the part of her story where the writer says, "And she persuaded us." That makes me curious. How did she persuade them? How did she get Paul and his companions to agree to stay at her house? Was it that they were drawn to her bubbly excitement in her newfound faith in Christ? Or did she have a reputation as a great cook? (Personally, I think it was the latter, but I'll have to ask when I get to heaven.)

Lydia and the other women touched the lives of many through their generosity and hospitality. Some touched the lives of Jesus and his disciples, making their travels more comfortable and less worrisome. Others touched the lives of Paul and his coworkers, enabling them to continue in their ministry. In each case, their touch had a chain effect. Their care for these ministers enabled the ministers to touch the lives of others, who in turn touched the lives of others, and so on until this very day!

These women can also touch our lives by their example. Think about the women who were generous with their finances. How could you emulate their touch? Many missionaries must raise money to buy food, shelter, and the other necessities of life to sustain them while they're teaching unreached people about God's love. Could you contribute monthly to their support?

Or could you bless them in some other way? I've heard many sad stories from missionaries about the "gifts" they've received from churches back home—tattered clothing; worn, outdated books; broken toys for their children. Imagine the joy it would bring a missionary family to open a box and find brand-new clothes, recently published books with crisp pages and no underlining, games and toys still in their plastic wrap—or maybe even some nonperishable food items that aren't available where they're ministering. Now, *that* would be support!

Next, consider those Bible women who were generous with their homes. They gladly opened their doors to provide hospitality, comfort, and rest for those who were preaching and teaching about Christ. They weren't looking for anything in return; but oh, how they must have been blessed!

Did you know you can actually get a college degree and pursue a career in hospitality? Hospitality specialists are those people who manage restaurants, hotels, country clubs, and similar businesses. They get

paid to make people feel as comfortable and welcome in their estab-
lishment as they are in their own homes. In fact, I'm sure "make yourself at home" is the first thing they're taught to say in Hospitality 101.

We don't get paid a salary to open our homes to others, but we
certainly are rewarded with blessings. Think of Mary and Martha,
whose home was always open to Jesus; or Priscilla, who along with
her husband, Aquila, took in the apostle Paul. Not only did they get
to know their guests on a personal basis, they enjoyed the heartwarm-
ing feeling of knowing they were helping an important ministry go
on. As Jesus said, "Anyone who receives a prophet because he is a
prophet will receive a prophet's reward, and anyone who receives a
righteous man because he is a righteous man will receive a righteous
man's reward."[2]

Why not invite your pastor and his family over for dinner one
night? Why not offer that spare bedroom to a traveling speaker? These
are short-term commitments, but they show your support for these ministers and their work. Here are some other practical things you can do:

- wash their cars

- offer one night a month of free baby-sitting

- send notes of encouragement, mentioning specific ways you're
  thankful for their ministry

- stop by their office with donuts, a basket of fruit, or other
  edible goodies

- chip in toward a weekend getaway for them and their spouses

- remember and respect their day off

You probably can think of many other ideas. The key isn't just to
think them—it's to *do* them. Just as the women of the Bible were fur-
thering the ministry of Christ through their support, your touches of
support for your pastors, missionaries, and other ministers will be felt by
many. You'll touch not only them, but also everyone their ministries
touch. And I can't help thinking that if all of us would begin to show
our pastors this kind of practical support, that job description at the
beginning of the chapter would have a few more interested candidates!

Chapter Eight: The Hands of God

Lord, thank you for the men and women who devote themselves to serving you and us. Help me to be less critical of them and more supportive in all my words and actions.

"If you consider me a believer in the Lord," she said, "come and stay at my house." And she persuaded us.

—Acts 16:15

Chapter Nine

TOUCH AND GO

Random Touches Both Near and Far

All of this has been to say thank you for answering God's call to write books.
Your obedience is one of the main reasons why I am alive and serving God today.
—formerly suicidal young woman

Scrubbing or Scrawling?

Robin first began to think of a career as a missionary while attending a Christian university. She heard missionaries speak in chapel. She attended Urbana, a huge missions conference held every few years in Illinois. She went forward in her church as a sign of commitment during Missions Emphasis Week. "I was ready, willing, and certain I would serve God best on the mission field," she remembers.

The only question was, where would she go? How would she serve?

"Once I filled out one of those placement applications that links you to different missions opportunities based on your skills and gifts," Robin explains. "The first one that came up for me was 'Laundry Supervisor, Kenya.' I cried. I thought, 'Are you sure this is the best way I can serve you, Lord—sorting laundry?' Then I read Brother Lawrence's classic book, *The Practice of the Presence of God*, and I understood that we are all called to be servants. If I could do that best in a laundry room in Kenya, so be it."

With a smile, Robin adds, "But God had something else in mind."

Robin married a youth pastor. (Some would say that's a mission field in itself!) "We took mission trips to Mexico each year," says Robin, "and we encouraged a number of young people to go into missions. I thought perhaps that was my ultimate role in fulfilling the Great Commission—prompting others to go since I hadn't. I always wondered if I had fully obeyed God since I hadn't gone into 'all the world' as I had thought I would."

While working with teenagers alongside her husband, Robin learned that many of the girls in the youth group loved to read romance novels. Unfortunately, there were few books in that genre that were written from a Christian perspective. So, encouraged by the group, Robin began writing. And to her surprise, Christian girls everywhere began to read what she wrote.

Since then, Robin has written more than forty books, including the popular Christy Miller series, the Sierra Jensen series, and the Glenbrooke series. These stories are read by women and girls all over the world, including such far-flung places as Brazil, Sweden, Thailand, New Zealand, Romania, Latvia, and Austria—not to mention all over the United States. Perhaps you or your daughter have read one of the many books by Robin Jones-Gunn.

What about her dreams of the mission field? "One day it became clear: *This* is what God wanted all along—to multiply like the loaves and fishes, to feed a multitude," she says. "At first I thought that writing stories for teens was a lesser calling than going to the mission field. Writing books didn't seem nearly as dramatic as taking a canoe to the remote jungles of Papua, New Guinea, and translating the Scriptures into a previously unwritten language. Yet this was the call God had on my life and the way he uniquely gifted me to serve him. And he gets all the glory."[1]

Through Robin's obedience, she has touched the lives of literally millions of girls, most of whom she will never meet. These are random touches, aimed not at specific individuals but at anyone who happens to pick up one of her books. Robin has no control over who these people will be. Yet letters regularly pour into her home, written by young women who excitedly relate how Robin's touch has been multiplied by God to change their lives. Here—misspellings and all—is a sampling of those touches:

I have a Hindu indian friend who has being reading your books. And just because of her reading them she has being asking a lot of questions about christianity. She even now says she wants to get married in a christian church. One of her questions was why don't I believe in sex before marriage?

I am so thankful that you wrote this book about that subject (when I say subject I am referring to how Sierra is too obsessed over Paul). It is just what I need to get my heart back on track with God.

Chapter Nine: Touch and Go

Four years ago I became a Christian even though my parents are Buddists. I felt that I wasn't a real Christian because I couldn't go to church and I didn't have a Bible...until I read your book. Christy and Todd really changed my perspective of God and being a Christian and they told me that God was real and he was a true friend who would never forsake you.

The Christy Miller Series was my inspiration to follow Christ. My walk with God has not been the same since I started reading your books. After reading *Sunsets*, my questions were becoming clearer and I knew that I could not give up on God because he has never given up on me. I started reading my devotions and praying every night before I went to bed. Since getting back into my walk with God and reading your books, my whole life has been turned around.

I am a 15 year old girl. I was doing the rebellion thing, staying out late, partying, doing drugs, drinking, smoking, etc. I was a Christian. But, I was backsliding, bad. I bought your book for a book report I had to do at school. I have learned more about God, from this one book, than 15 years of church.

Last Christmas my mom gave me the first four of the Christy Miller Series. After I read them (this is the cool part!) GUESS WHAT! Those four books touched my heart so much that I gave my heart to God!

It was through your book *Summer Promise* that I was explained the process of salvation and I became a Christian when Christy gave her heart to the Lord...The books always encourage me to pray in times of trouble.

God used you to save my life. At only 13 years of age, I began plotting my suicide...Something kept stopping me from ending my life. It seemed as though a little voice was continuously whispering, 'There is hope. Don't give up. I love you.' I now know that the voice belonged to God, who made himself real to me through your books. The love of God, portrayed in each book, cried out to the deepest needs of my heart...I am finally complete in Christ and am seeking only his will for my life.

As Romans 11:29 reminds us, God has given us gifts, and he's given us a purpose. It's really up to us to be obedient and to listen and follow God's course for our lives instead of our own. Are you doing this?

Some people script out their lives. "I'm going to get married when I'm twenty-four and have my first of three children (one boy, two girls) at age twenty-six. I'll set aside five years for raising the kids and getting them into preschool, then I'll get back on track with my high-power career. I'll earn enough money to buy a big house, a new car, and a fashionable wardrobe. Then, when I retire on schedule at sixty-two, I'll volunteer at church and do gardening. And I'll stay a size 5 the entire time." There are a few rare women who manage to follow these scripts, but more often than not, God throws some curves into our lives to make sure we're following his plan and not ours. God also throws in a few people whose lives we can touch along the way.

Take time to listen to God. What's his script for your life? Are you open to whatever direction he gives? You could become a laundry worker in Kenya—or the laundry supervisor in your own house. You could be like Robin, touching many lives far away through a ministry like writing, or you could touch lives closer to home by supporting local ministries to the poor and hurting. Either way, following God's course instead of your own is likely to mean stepping out of your comfort zone at times. You need an open mind and a willing heart to stay flexible in the hands of God.

Robin Jones-Gunn has allowed God to extend her touch beyond her immediate realm. She has used her gifts for the purpose he intended—and has impacted lives beyond her wildest dreams. And it sounds like she's gotten out of doing a lot of laundry in the bargain! I can't promise you anything about that pile of dirty clothes in your laundry room. But I can guarantee that if you use the gifts God has given you for the purposes he opens up for you, you, too, will impact lives in ways you never imagined.

Lord, let me truly call you my Lord and follow with obedience no matter where you lead.

For God's gifts and his call are irrevocable.
—Romans 11:29

Your smile spreads like a butterfly.
—Mario Ruoppolo in *Il Postino*

Smile!

Are you "on-line"? Personally, I love the way the Internet has enabled me to keep in touch with friends and family from all over the country. E-mail is simple, and it's fun! In addition to sending personal messages, many of my friends forward interesting stories, news items, jokes, poems, and other engaging tidbits to me via the Internet. These items tend to hop from friend to friend and computer to computer until, eventually, their original source is impossible to trace.

I told you about one of them back in chapter 6—remember the advice on happy homemaking from the 1950s home-economics book? Recently another story came through that I knew I had to share with you. I don't know how long it has been making the rounds from computer to computer. I don't know the author's name. I don't even know if the story is true. But I hope it is, because the message is wonderful!

It seems a mother of three was taking a sociology class on the way to completing her college degree. At the end of the semester, the instructor assigned a project called "Smile" in which class members were required to go out and smile at three strangers, then record the strangers' reactions. Soon afterward, the woman found herself waiting in line with her husband and youngest son at the local McDonald's. Suddenly she noticed that the people around her were backing away from the counter. Even her husband took a few steps back. Feeling a sense of panic, she turned to see what was causing the commotion.

Her nose picked up the reason before her eyes did. Two ragged, homeless men had approached the line, and the odor of unwashed bodies and dirty clothes was overpowering.

Somehow the woman managed to hold her ground. Then, looking into the kindly blue eyes of the shorter of the two men, she noticed that he was smiling. "Good day," he said to her as he counted out his coins. Then she glanced at the second man, who was fumbling with his hands and appeared to be mentally deficient. She was strangely touched as she realized that the shorter man was doing all he could to take care of his dependent friend. She held back a sudden urge to reach out and hug him.

When the blue-eyed man stepped forward to place his order, he asked only for coffee. That was all he could afford. But at least he'd made a purchase, and now he and his friend could sit for a while in the restaurant and escape the cold March air.

As the woman watched the men shuffle away, she stepped up to the counter, suddenly aware that everyone in the restaurant was looking at her. She was the only one who hadn't recoiled from the two homeless souls. What was she going to do now? She writes, "I smiled and asked the young lady behind the counter to give me two more breakfast meals on a separate tray. I then walked around the corner to the table that the men had chosen as a resting spot. I put the tray on the table and laid my hand on the blue-eyed gentleman's cold hand. He looked up at me with tears in his eyes and said, 'Thank you.'

"I leaned over, began to pat his hand, and said, 'I did not do this for you. God is here working through me to give you hope.' I started to cry as I walked away to join my husband and son."

When the woman returned to college and turned in her project, the instructor shared her story with the rest of the class. "In my own way," she says in retrospect, "I had touched the people at McDonald's, my husband, son, instructor, and every soul that shared the classroom on the last night I spent as a college student. I graduated with one of the biggest lessons I would ever learn: unconditional acceptance."[2]

This woman's story is a beautiful example of a random touch. There are people we encounter each day for only a brief moment—the clerk at the department store, the young mother in the doctor's waiting room, the gentleman standing at the bus stop. We didn't plan to see them. We will likely never meet them again. But as this woman at McDonald's makes so perfectly clear, every touch matters, no matter how fleeting. She was an example of God's love not only to the two homeless men, but also to every person who saw or heard what she did.

Random, fleeting touches do make a difference—for good or not so good. If someone in the grocery store line is rude to you, you are more likely to start feeling rude and snap at the next person you meet, right? But if someone greets you instead with a smile and a happy wink, you're more likely to pass along a cheerier sentiment.

Romans 16:16 tells us to greet one another with a holy kiss. This instruction is repeated five times in the Bible.[3] Obviously, God thinks it's important that we approach the people we meet with a happy, loving touch.

I'm not going to suggest that you go around kissing everyone you meet. These days, you'd probably get into a bit of trouble (although some people might welcome a good smooch!). Instead of kisses, try smiles. In fact, take that instructor's "Smile" project a bit further. Don't just smile at three people; smile at everyone you meet for a whole week. See if it makes a difference in how they react to you—and how they react to others.

Start a chain of cheer and watch how far it goes. Who knows—maybe your smile today will start a chain reaction that will inspire someone to smile at someone, who will smile at someone, who will smile at me tomorrow. I'd like that. And I promise I'll smile back!

Father, smile on me with your love so that I, in turn, might smile on others.

Greet one another with a holy kiss.
—Romans 16:16

Stop, look, and listen!
—Jiminy Cricket, "Stop, Look, and Listen"

People Watchers

I'm a people watcher from way back. Ever since I was a little girl I've loved to go to a mall or an airport and just sit and watch people go about their daily lives. Now my family has picked up my passion. Whenever a delayed flight strands us at an airline gate, we pass the time by making up stories about the people who walk by. We try to name the celebrities we think they look like or guess where they're going based on their attire. It's a fun way to amuse ourselves.

The truth is, people are watching us all the time—and it's surprising how much they can learn just by watching. I remember being in an airport once with my grandmother, waiting for a family member to arrive on the next flight. I was only ten, but I already loved people-watching. Suddenly I burst into laughter. A woman leaving the nearby rest room had the entire backside of her dress tucked into her pantyhose! I thought this was hysterical, but my grandmother, following my gaze, was mortified. She rushed over to the woman to rescue her from further embarrassment.

I did learn something from that people-watching session: Always check the mirror before going out in public! This woman whose name I'll never know made a random, spontaneous touch on my life. Not only did she provide me with a good laugh (hey, I was just a kid!), but she taught me an important grooming lesson. She touched my life without even knowing it.

I can think of two women in the Bible who were being watched by others, even though they never planned on an audience. The first was a poor widow who went to the Jewish temple in Jerusalem. While the rich folks, with great fanfare, were tossing large amounts of money into the temple treasury, this seemingly insignificant woman dropped in two copper coins worth only about a fraction of a cent. She didn't know that Jesus and his disciples were people-watching that day—or that Jesus was going to use her as an object lesson. But after seeing her sacrifice, Jesus said, "I tell you the truth, this poor widow has put more into the treasury than all the others. They all gave out of their wealth; but she, out of her poverty, put in everything—all she had to live on."[4]

This widow could have put only one coin into the temple coffers. She could have put in nothing, and no one would have blamed her— she was so incredibly poor. But she gave sacrificially, and Jesus noticed. She certainly had no idea that her actions were going to be recorded in the Bible. She had no way of knowing her gift would go down as one of the most generous in Christian history. Her actions were simply a reflection of what was in her heart. Others saw and learned from her example.

The second woman who was watched was Mary, the sister of Martha and Lazarus. Her story is told in three of the Gospels. Let's read the account in Matthew 26:6–13:

> While Jesus was in Bethany in the home of a man known as Simon the Leper, a woman came to him with an alabaster jar of very expensive perfume, which she poured on his head as he was reclining at the table.
>
> When the disciples saw this, they were indignant. "Why this waste?" they asked. "This perfume could have been sold at a high price and the money given to the poor."
>
> Aware of this, Jesus said to them, "Why are you bothering this woman? She has done a beautiful thing to me. The poor you will always have with you, but you will not always have me. When she poured this perfume on my body, she did it to prepare me for burial. I tell you the truth, wherever this gospel is preached throughout the world, what she has done will also be told, in memory of her."

Mary's only intention was to express her love for Jesus. Maybe the perfume was her way of thanking him for raising her brother from the dead. Maybe she understood that Jesus would be giving up his life in the very near future, and she wanted to declare her devotion to him while she still could. Like the woman with the two coins, she wasn't trying to put on a show. She wasn't playing to an audience. She just wanted Jesus to be honored.

John's account of this event tells us that the person who cried in protest over the "waste" of this expensive gift was Judas Iscariot—the treasurer of the group and the disciple who would ultimately betray Jesus. The Bible says, "He did not say this because he cared about the poor but because he was a thief; as keeper of the money bag, he used to help himself to what was put into it."[5] But Jesus saw through Judas's false indignation. Jesus understood what Mary had done, and he declared that the story of her sacrificial gift would be told for centuries to come.

These two Bible women loved God to the best of their ability; they held nothing back in lavishing their devotion upon him. They didn't realize that people were watching them and recording their actions. They had no idea their examples would touch millions of people over many centuries, teaching a timeless lesson on true sacrificial giving. Their touches were random, rippling down through history in ways they never expected, impacting people they never would meet.

Yet their touches remain powerful. You and I can still be touched by these women—even though they never planned it that way. We can still learn from them.

The obvious lesson is that we need to give our all to God. We need to give to him out of the abundance of our heart—not our pocketbook. When you give your money, your talents, or your time, are you giving out of an overflow of thankfulness and love, recognizing that God made the ultimate sacrifice when he gave his only son to pay for your sins and mine?

A second lesson is this: People are always watching. In your home, at work, in your neighborhood, when you're gathered with friends—literally, everywhere you go—people are watching you. The actions you think you are doing in secret may one day be broadcast to a much larger audience. Are those actions ones that honor God and demonstrate your love for him? Would you want others to follow your example?

Commit today to stop holding back from God. Love him with everything that's within you. And do it as if Jesus were the only one in the audience! Yes, people are watching—but you don't have to put on a show. If you love the Lord with all your heart, people will notice, and they will follow.

Lord, as I strive to follow you, help me to be a shining example even in the smallest of actions.

The eyes of the LORD are everywhere, keeping watch on the wicked and the good.
—Proverbs 15:3

As you pour out your love on someone else, it will boomerang back to you.
—Barbara Johnson, "Splashes of Joy"

A Random Touch of Kindness

Barbara Johnson often wears a button that says, "Someone Jesus loves has AIDS." If you didn't know her, you might think it strange to see this well-groomed and matronly woman wearing such a pin. But Barbara isn't what she appears. Life has not been a walk in the park (or a skip through the department store). No bed of roses for her! No, Barbara's a survivor. She's gone through the deaths of two of her sons. Another son lived for years as a homosexual. Out of her pain, she began Spatula Ministries—designed, as she says, to "scrape parents off the ceiling" when their lives go awry.

These days Barbara also adds writing and speaking with the Women of Faith conferences to her "to do" list. It was at one of these conferences that she was able to save a woman's life through a random, spontaneous touch.

Barbara had just finished her turn at the podium, sharing about her "Someone Jesus loves has AIDS" button and how hard it can be to truly live our lives asking "What would Jesus do?" As she was escorted to another room for lunch, the conference director rushed up to her. In an urgent tone she explained that a woman named Toni was in the coliseum and was threatening to commit suicide unless Barbara met with her right away.

Toni was a prostitute with AIDS, hiding from her pimp who'd already shot and cut her. She had taken refuge in a Dumpster overnight and had ended up at the coliseum the next day, where a kind woman had given her a ticket to get in to the conference. She had listened to Barbara share about Jesus' love for everyone, even those with AIDS—and now she was desperate to talk to her.

Barbara and many of the Women of Faith staffers raced to a locker room where Toni was waiting. Then Barbara and Toni began to talk, and Toni poured out the story of her hard life. "Toni said she desperately wanted to get out of her life in prostitution," Barbara recalls. "She wanted to become a Christian, but she had to get away from her pimp." Barbara gave Toni one of her "Someone Jesus loves has AIDS" buttons, and Toni pinned it onto her filthy shirt while the women continued to encourage her. "We reminded her that Jesus loved her," Barbara says, "and that she could have a new heart and a new life. She obviously grasped these ideas wholeheartedly, and right then and there she prayed with us to accept Christ as her Savior. We all jubilantly joined her in saying a loud 'Amen!'"

The women scrambled to find soap, towels, and clean clothes for Toni. They collected enough money for her to buy a bus ticket to Chicago where her family lived and could help her. Toni emerged from the locker room looking like a new woman on the outside—just as she truly was on the inside. Barbara knew that no matter what happened, Toni had a new life ahead of her. If she made it to safety in Chicago, her family could help her start over. But even if her pimp tracked her down and killed her, she would find herself in the arms of Jesus.

Someone drove Toni to the bus depot, and Barbara never heard from her again. Her touch on the young woman had lasted only a brief moment, as the world counts time—but in God's time, it was eternal. And Toni wasn't the only one impacted by Barbara's random touch. The other women who'd been involved in counseling Toni had never "had the opportunity to embrace such a down-and-out person, a woman with AIDS who came out of a Dumpster to touch their lives. Some of them may not even have known what a pimp is, and they had certainly never embraced a prostitute! But there they were, ministering to her with love and concern, praying for her, hugging her, and sending her off with great sympathy for her needs."

The security guards and police who had been called to the emergency also witnessed the scene, some with tears in their eyes. They wouldn't quickly forget what they saw! Their lives, too, were changed by Barbara's touch.[6]

For Barbara Johnson, that's par for the course. She touches many people—often without planning to—just by making herself available to whomever God happens to bring her way. She knows the value of a touch, even if it's just a brief one.

In fact, for more than seven years now, Barbara has set aside the month of December to personally call grieving parents on the telephone, talking for just a few minutes to each person who contacted Spatula Ministries that year because they lost a child. From her California home, she begins making calls to the East Coast at 4:30 in the morning, then moves west through the time zones. She listens to these parents' sorrow, lets them know she cares, and prays with them. In December of 1999, she made more than five hundred calls! Each call is relatively brief, but Barbara feels she can bring a little bit of joy to hurting lives through this quick touch through the telephone lines.[7]

Are you keeping your eyes and ears open for people who might need a spontaneous touch of the love of God—through you? Are you available if God brings them your way? They might be dirty and ragged. They might be sick and scared. Touching them might make you uncomfortable, put you outside your comfort zone. But ask yourself: What would Jesus do? What would Jesus want *you* to do?

Don't underestimate the value of a touch, however brief. You might just change a life for eternity.

Heavenly Father, guide me to those who need you. Give me compassion and an understanding of what you want my response to be.

Let your compassion come to me that I may live.
—Psalm 119:77

Winnie-isms

Have you noticed how kids pick up the phrases, expressions, and gestures of their parents? My mother uses a number of colorful expressions or sayings. For example, when she's driving behind a slow car, she grumbles, "Milk it or move it, buster." If she accidentally pops the clutch or someone darts in front of her, she exclaims, "Hold 'er, Newt! She's headin' for the barn!" When my dad can't find the peanut butter and she walks over to the cabinet and points right to it, she comments, "If it was a snake, it 'a jumped out an' bit ya."

I don't know where all these sayings come from. Maybe you've heard some of them too. But since my mom's name is Winnie, my family calls them "Winnie-isms." What's especially funny to me is hearing my son use these expressions after he's spent a week with Grandma. She doesn't try to teach Tony these phrases; he just picks them up from being around her. He's listening to her when she doesn't even know it.

In the last few chapters we've noted that people are watching us. They're listening to us, too, and what they hear can impact them—for better or for worse.

I remember the day I stood to make a presentation for my fifth-grade class. About halfway through the teacher interrupted me and began to mimic me with an exaggerated lisp. My classmates laughed, but I was mortified. Did I have a lisp? Did I really sound that way when I talked? Why hadn't someone told me? I was overcome by a tidal wave of embarrassment and self-doubt—and to this day I wonder if I'm speaking clearly enough when I address large groups. Friends have assured me that I don't lisp, but the unkind comments of that teacher have stuck with me for years.

In college I had a more positive experience with words. One afternoon a friend and I picked a bucket of berries and went to his aunt's house to make a pie. His aunt was a wonderful cook, and she was known especially for making great desserts. When she tasted a slice of our masterpiece, she raved, "This pie crust is delicious!" Her random, spontaneous comment made my heart swell with pride.

About fifteen years later, I saw this woman again and told her how much that one comment had meant to me. She didn't remember saying it! No matter. To this day I have a reputation for making good pies—largely because of the confidence that came from one fleeting comment from a woman I admired.

The words that come out of our mouths make a difference. They touch people as surely as our hands do. And sometimes, they override any other impression we intend to give. You've probably seen a beautiful woman at one time or another and been astounded by her magazine-perfect looks. Then she opened her mouth, and out came utterances so crude you quickly clapped your hands over the ears of a nearby child. She could have touched you with her beauty. Instead she touched you with vulgarity. How sad!

Our words have the power to shape how others see us. They have the power to build others up with encouragement. They also have the power to tear them down with judgment and criticism. Think of the way you talk to the people around you—your family, your friends, your coworkers, your acquaintances, even the strangers you connect with for only a few moments. What kind of touch are you making with your words?

As you consider your answer, reflect on these words from the Bible:

Not a word from their mouth can be trusted; their heart is filled with destruction. Their throat is an open grave; with their tongue they speak deceit. (Psalm 5:9)

May the words of my mouth and the meditation of my heart be pleasing in your sight, O LORD, my Rock and my Redeemer. (Psalm 19:14)

My mouth speaks what is true, for my lips detest wickedness. All the words of my mouth are just; none of them is crooked or perverse. (Proverbs 8:7–8)

A gentle answer turns away wrath, but a harsh word stirs up anger. (Proverbs 15:1)

Words from a wise man's mouth are gracious, but a fool is consumed by his own lips. (Ecclesiastes 10:12)

For out of the overflow of the heart the mouth speaks. (Matthew 12:34)

Therefore encourage each other with these words. (1 Thessalonians 4:18)

With the tongue we praise our Lord and Father, and with it we curse men, who have been made in God's likeness. Out of the same mouth come praise and cursing. My brothers, this should not be. (James 3:9–10)

The Bible speaks a great deal about our words because God knows how powerful words can be. After all, the world came into being by his word. Jesus came to the earth as God's "word" to the human race. He knows that the tongue can be like the rudder of a ship, steering our lives—and the lives of others—toward blessing or toward destruction. The choice is ours.[8]

When I think about my mom and her Winnie-isms, I also think of all the good and kind words that have come out of her mouth over the years—words that have encouraged me, given me hope, and made me feel loved and appreciated. To me, these are the *real* Winnie-isms. Not only have they shown me my mother's heart, they have touched me and shaped me into the woman I am today. For these words, I am forever grateful.

What are the words you will be remembered for—words of gossip or words of grace? Will your lips pour out destructive curses or bathe others in healing words of love? Will you spout verbal abuse or verbal applause? Rest assured: What's in your heart *will* come out through your lips, and others will be touched by those words.

Are you listening to yourself? What do you hear?

Chapter Nine: Touch and Go

Heavenly Father, fill my heart with love, and let it pour out through my mouth as praise to you and encouragement to others.

May our Lord Jesus Christ himself and God our Father, who loved us and by his grace gave us eternal encouragement and good hope, encourage your hearts and strengthen you in every good deed and word.
—2 Thessalonians 2:16–17

Chapter Ten

I'M TOUCHED

Touching Your Own Heart

People get ready...Jesus is comin'.
—Crystal Lewis, "People Get Ready...Jesus Is Comin'"

A Ready Defense

"Hi-Ya!"

Yes, that's me giving my best imitation of a karate-chop yell. Are you impressed? Actually, I'm not doing karate; I'm doing tae kwon do, a Korean martial art. And I'm not getting ready to chop; I'm about to throw a kick. Minor technicalities!

When my son first began taking tae kwon do, I did the "mom-as-chauffeur" thing. I drove him to each class then sat and read a book while he jumped, kicked, and generally got sweaty. But after several months of peeking over the pages to watch from the sidelines, I decided to join him. I would get some exercise, I figured, and I might learn a little bit about self-defense. I'd also have a new area of interest to share with Tony. So I took off my shoes, stepped onto the mat, and began to jump, kick—and sweat a whole lot.

Most people join a tae kwon do class to learn various kicks, blocks, punches, and other defensive moves. And there are certainly plenty of those. But students have to learn many other things as well—like Korean history and the names of various generals and war heroes. I've had to memorize fact upon fact upon fact until my brain has swum. I've even had to learn to count in Korean.

As in any school, this one has pop quizzes and tests. When every-one is lined up at attention and the instructor calls on a student to explain a piece of history or demonstrate a series of moves, we all feel the tension in the air. If the student makes a mistake, the instructor can choose to correct the answer and graciously excuse the error or apply discipline in the form of extra push-ups or some other exercise.

Sometimes the whole class is made to suffer for the inaccurate answer, and everyone has to do the extra exercises.

You can understand, then, why I take my homework fairly seriously! I study my history pages and practice my moves in every free moment—while I wait for my turn in the bathroom, say, or while I'm watching the microwave timer count down to dinnertime. I don't want to be called on and make an error. I don't want to do extra push-ups. And most importantly, I don't want to be approached by a stranger in a dark parking lot and not feel prepared to defend myself. I want to be ready!

Over the years I've avoided most organized sports because the training has always looked so grueling. And I've often winced when I've heard young people in the military talk about the rigors of boot camp; the effort required seems excessive, even cruel! Yet more and more I'm learning why the drills and exercises are necessary. Athletes, soldiers, and others in training want to be ready for the challenges they will face.

My instructor might be surprised to hear this, but my tae kwon do lessons have taught me a great deal about my training as a woman of God. When I'm called on to defend what I believe, I need to be ready. When a situation confronts me, I must be prepared to take action.

How am I going to respond to people who are critical of my faith in Jesus Christ? Am I going to react in love or in anger? Will I touch them in a way that will cause them to think—and maybe even change their life for the better? What would Jesus want me to do?

That last question is the biggie. And the only way I'm going to know the answer is by knowing Jesus and knowing his Word. I study my martial arts lessons because I want to be ready both in class and on the street. I should be even more diligent in studying the Word of God and getting to know Jesus so I'll be ready for any situation he brings my way.

Being ready involves several components. For one, we need to have a good working knowledge of the Bible so we can answer a question or enter a discussion with confidence. We don't want to hem and haw with lame statements like, "You'll just have to trust me—I know there's a verse somewhere in the Bible that talks about that!" I'm not saying we have to memorize the entire Bible, but we do need to read it, think about what we've read, and let the words of God soak into our hearts and minds. Then we'll be ready to touch others with words of truth.

We also need to be ready to talk about our faith and our personal walk with God when others ask us to "give the reason for the hope that [we] have," as 1 Peter 3:15 says. I learned this lesson the hard way. When I was in high school, I was always a bit early for one of my classes, so I often chatted with the instructor before my classmates arrived. One day he said, "There's something different about you. You've always got a smile on your face. Why is that?"

What an opportune moment! This was my big chance to share my faith with my teacher. He was practically begging me to tell him about the joy of knowing Jesus!

"Oh, I don't know. I guess I just have an optimistic attitude most of the time," I responded lamely.

Thud—that's the sound my heart made as it fell into my shoes. Because I had never really thought about how I'd answer such a question, I floundered terribly when I was put on the spot. I missed a wonderful opportunity to touch this man with the love of Jesus because I wasn't prepared.

A third component of being ready is making sure our own hearts are touched and changed by God. We've got to take care of our own lives—touch our own hearts, you might say—if we are going to be effective in touching others. Unfortunately, we often overlook this simple truth.

What is the condition of your heart? Does it need some attention? Have you been so busy giving to others that your well is running dry? Are you truly prepared? Let's spend the remainder of this book exploring how to touch our own hearts so we're ready for action when challenges arise.

A Ready Defense

Lord, open my eyes to my own condition. Help me to examine my heart and do whatever it takes to make sure I'm ready when you call me to touch others.

But in your hearts set apart Christ as Lord.
Always be prepared to give an answer to everyone who asks you to give the reason for the hope that you have.
—1 Peter 3:15

Fill 'er Up

I doubt there is anyone in America who doesn't remember the horrifying events of April 20, 1999, when two teenage boys opened fire at Columbine High School near Denver, Colorado. Living only about fifty miles from the site of this monstrous assault, Mike, Tony, and I prayed and prayed for those involved, searching the newscasts for names and pictures of anyone we knew.

The pain of Columbine did not end with the shootings. Since that awful day, lawsuit upon lawsuit has been filed against the parents of the boys responsible, against the school, and against the law enforcement officials. Memorials have been defaced, removed, or disallowed. The mother of one student who survived the Columbine attack committed suicide—apparently the strain of coping in the aftermath of the attack was too much. We may never know the full extent of the misery caused by this terrible crime.

A few glimmers of hope and joy have shined through, however. One of these is the story of Cassie Bernall, the teenager who reportedly said yes when the gunman asked if she believed in God—and who was shot after giving that answer. Teens and adults alike have hailed Cassie as a modern-day martyr. Her simple words have touched the lives of countless people with hope and courage.

Another story isn't getting as much press: the story of Crystal Woodman. Crystal was a friend of Cassie's. The girls not only attended the same school, they were part of the same church youth group and even volunteered together at a homeless shelter. Crystal was also in the library the day of the shootings, hiding under a table and fervently praying to God, "Send your angels down." She escaped with her life—and her memories.

Certainly, Crystal's life has been permanently changed by the Columbine tragedy. But unlike the many finger pointers and blame finders who've come out of the woodwork since the assault, Crystal has chosen a path of forgiveness and healing. Just before Christmas, several months after the shooting, seventeen-year-old Crystal prepared to board a plane to Kosovo. As part of "Operation Christmas Child," she was traveling to this war-torn country to touch impoverished children with the love of God.

Operation Christmas Child is a ministry of Samaritan's Purse, an international relief organization run by Franklin Graham. Around Christmastime, people from all across America fill shoeboxes with small toys, books, toiletry items, clothing, gospel literature, and other age-appropriate items. The boxes are collected, wrapped, and delivered to needy children throughout the world. Literally millions of boxes are given out each year. In December 1999, Crystal Woodman was helping to deliver some of the 81,450 boxes donated by people in her home state.

Crystal says that on that terrible day in the Columbine library, she caught a glimpse of what life is like for many of the world's children. "I got a chance to experience terror and fear and hopelessness," she says. "But I rose above it, I got through it, and I now have hope that maybe sometime down the road, everything will be OK again. That's what I am going to share with these kids in Kosovo."

Crystal emerged from Columbine with a strong sense of mission. "God has blessed my life," she says, "and saw fit to spare me in the library. I think he knew I could derive strength from him and use that to help others, to show love and compassion to those who need it, too."

God has blessed my life. Could you say such a thing after seeing several of your friends murdered? After watching the media have a heyday at the expense of families you know are in pain? When you're having frequent nightmares of guns and blood? While lawsuits, arguments, and hurt feelings are still running rampant? Obviously Crystal made some strong choices about how she was going to live from that point on. "I am moving past this," she explains, relating that it's her faith in God that has helped her choose and follow this path.[1]

I know people with faith in God who still harbor bitterness in their hearts over events that occurred many years before. These Christians can't let go of past hurts and offenses. They are angry at others, themselves, and God—and their bitterness pours out on everyone around them. These unhappy people have chosen a different path than Crystal.

God has told us in the Bible that we must forgive. We must not hold on to offenses. We must cast all our burdens on him. If we don't, we will suffer for it—and so will all the people in our lives.

Whatever is in your heart will come out in times of trouble. Matthew 12:34 says, "For out of the overflow of the heart the mouth speaks." Just as coffee overflows and spills when you jostle the cup, the contents of your heart overflow and spill when you are jostled in life. And just as coffee leaves a stain on a tablecloth, anger and hatred stain the hearts of all the people you touch, leaving indelible and unsightly marks. The good news is that love and mercy stain too—but in a beautiful and welcome way. Which kind of stain are you leaving behind?

Make a choice today to pour out the bitter dregs of unforgiveness and fill the cup of your life with love and mercy. Are there people who've made you angry? Are you holding a grudge? Do you sense a deep bitterness eating away inside?

As it was for Crystal Woodman, your choice must be intentional and sure. You must choose to forgive and allow God to help you. Only when your cup is filled with love, mercy, hope, and forgiveness will you be able to offer these blessings to others out of your overflow.

Merciful Father, help me to forgive others as you have forgiven me. Fill the cup of my heart with love and mercy so that blessing will spill out in the shaky times of life.

May the God of hope fill you with all joy and peace
as you trust in him, so that you may overflow with hope by the
power of the Holy Spirit.
—Romans 15:13

Humans are very seldom either totally sincere or totally hypocritical.
Their moods change, their motives are mixed,
and they are often themselves quite mistaken as to what their motives are.
—C. S. Lewis in *The Quotable Lewis*

Fingers Crossed

When I was in college I knew a guy who wanted nothing more than to lead people to Christ. That sounds noble—but his motive was unusual. He was determined to be the person with the most crowns in heaven, and he figured he would earn a crown for every person he convinced to believe in Jesus. Talk about a competitive spirit! On the one hand, it's great that this guy was sharing about Jesus with literally everyone he met. On the other hand, it's sad that his motives were purely selfish. He didn't care about the people he was talking to. He was in it for his own glory!

Have you ever done this same kind of thing? Oh, you probably weren't so blatant, but your motives were just as fishy! Be honest. Maybe you volunteered to organize a fund-raising project in your community just so everyone would praise you for doing a great job. You didn't have an interest in the people or the cause that needed the funds—you just wanted your friends and neighbors to pat you on the back and look at you with admiration.

Or maybe you invited a coworker to your house and spent the hours before she arrived cleaning and cooking up a storm. You stressed and strained over every detail just to impress her. You didn't care about her, her needs, her concerns, the trials of her life. You just wanted her to think better of you and to admire your nice things. Believe me, I'm not pointing fingers. I'm guilty too—although I've learned from experience it's better to have a dirty house and a clean heart than the other way around. (The dirty house is the easy part!)

If you're saying "ouch" along with me, we have some good Bible company. Martha, the friend of Jesus whose story is told in Luke 10, was more concerned about making sure everyone was impressed with her home and her cooking than about making herself available to receive what Jesus had to offer. (My sister Jody calls her "Martha Stewart" because she was so concerned with being the "perfect" homemaker.) But when Martha told Jesus to tell Mary to stop sitting at his feet and start helping her with the housework, Jesus gently corrected her. "'Martha, Martha,' the Lord answered, 'you are worried and upset about many things, but only one thing is needed. Mary has chosen what is better, and it will not be taken away from her.'"[2]

As this story illustrates, there's a time to be busy and a time to be still; a time to serve and a time to be served; a time to think of others and a time to think of ourselves. That's not a license to be selfish and conceited, putting ourselves above others. Nor is it permission to shirk our responsibilities in order to spend every waking moment studying the Bible. However, it *is* a challenge to evaluate where we stand in our relationship with God and to consider what our motives are in touching the people around us.

We find a pretty straightforward admonition in the first few verses of 1 Corinthians 13: "If I speak in the tongues of men and of angels, but have not love, I am only a resounding gong or a clanging cymbal. If I have the gift of prophecy and can fathom all mysteries and all knowledge, and if I have a faith that can move mountains, but have not love, I am nothing. If I give all I possess to the poor and surrender my body to the flames, but have not love, I gain nothing."[3]

The truth is, we can have incredible talents and abilities. We can discover the cure for cancer or land a spaceship on Mars. But if we don't have love, our achievements are hollow. We can donate our paychecks to the poor, spend our evenings working in soup kitchens and homeless shelters, and volunteer for every church function imaginable. But if our motives are anything but love, we gain nothing of eternal value.

Without love as our motivation, we're just like the guy back in college who was winning souls for his own glory. Sure, it's great that people were coming to Christ. And it's great when we volunteer, use our talents, and find ways to help those in need. But without God's love in our hearts, we're doing these things for our own selfish motives.

We're pointing people toward us—saying by our actions, "Look at me! Aren't you impressed?" Instead, our touch should be pointing people to Christ. The glory is rightfully his!

Take time now to reread those verses in 1 Corinthians 13 and think about why you want to touch the lives of others. Is it because you love God and want to pass his love on? Or is it because you want people to think you're a great person? Are you touching lives because you love the individuals you're reaching out to? Or are you touching them because you want a pat on the back or to look better in their eyes?

Examine your motives. If love isn't at the heart of them, stop your busyness this instant and spend some good, quality time with God. You'll be glad you did—and so will all the people whose lives you will touch.

Loving God, you know me better than I know myself. Wash every selfish and impure motive from my heart and help me to touch others with nothing but your love.

Love is patient, love is kind. It does not envy, it does not boast, it is
not proud. It is not rude, it is not self-seeking, it is not easily
angered, it keeps no record of wrongs.
—1 Corinthians 13:4–5

Rogers, this is your queen speaking.
You will regain consciousness this instant.
—Queen Uberta in *The Swan Princess III*

God Saves the Queen

So much of the Old Testament reads like great drama, I often think its stories would make compelling movies, even in today's world of fast-paced, action-packed, special-effects-driven entertainment. Of course, Hollywood has already made some great films like the classic *The Ten Commandments* or the more recent animated feature *The Prince of Egypt*, both telling the story of Moses and the flight of the Israelites from Egyptian slavery. But other stories would be great on celluloid too—maybe even updated for a modern audience.

I'm thinking in particular of the story of Esther, documented in the book of the Bible by the same name. When I compare Esther's story to modern events in the worlds of politics, business, and entertainment, I can easily imagine a Hollywood update. Only a few minor changes would be necessary.

According to the Bible account, Esther was a Jewish orphan, taken in by a caring older cousin who raised her as his own daughter. The opening scene of our movie would show a darkened hospital room with a young Esther weeping over the loss of her parents. (Who would play the role of Esther? She would have to be someone strong, lovely, and talented; I suggest Gwyneth Paltrow.) Enter her dear cousin Mordecai (possibly Sean Connery?) who gathers her in his arms and leads her away. Time moves on…

Cut to a scene with Xerxes, the megazillionaire king of an unnamed country, and a rowdy bunch of men at a wild party. (Who would play Xerxes? He would have to be a handsome superstar—maybe Denzel Washington or Tom Cruise.) Liquor flows freely, the music is loud, and the laughter is raucous. Xerxes calls for his wife, Vashti (played by Whitney Houston, perhaps?), to come and dance before them all. She proudly refuses, and Xerxes is outraged.

"She refuses *me?* I'm the king!" he bellows.

"If this gets out, men throughout the kingdom will be reduced to nothing," his advisers sniff as they adjust their neckties. "Women won't have respect for any of us!" So head henchman Haman (only John Malkovich could do this villain justice) devises a plan...

Cut to Vashti being unceremoniously pushed out the front door of the castle, luggage in hand. Then cut to a newscaster giving the latest news flash: "A beauty contest is being held to find a new wife for Xerxes..." Women everywhere begin pounding on the doors of the TV station, preening and smiling for the cameras.

Back to Esther. She and Mordecai are playing some hoops together in the driveway of their modest home. One of Xerxes' advisers happens to drive by and notices her. Even in sweatpants and a ponytail, she's a knockout! He stops the car.

Fast forward now past the scenes where Esther marries Xerxes in a royal ceremony (you knew they'd get together!); where Mordecai saves Xerxes from a murderous scheme; and where the villain, Haman, becomes increasingly jealous of Mordecai's influence in the kingdom. Stop at the part where the evil Haman approaches Xerxes with a scheme to one-up his nemesis.

"Xerxes! I've just uncovered evidence that a group of people in the kingdom are planning a coup," he snarls. "It's the Jews—they're plotting a conspiracy against you!"

"Kill them all!" orders Xerxes as Haman turns away with a wicked smile.

Cut to the newscaster: "This just in. All people of Jewish descent will be put to death on December thirteenth." The camera pans over the anxious faces of crowds of Jews who cry and plead for a reprieve from stone-faced officials.

Meanwhile, Esther and Mordecai—both Jews, of course—secretly discuss a risky plan.

"This is why God allowed you to be chosen as queen," Mordecai gently explains. "You've got to save your people."

Chapter Ten: I'm Touched

"I'll do everything I can, even to the point of death," Esther bravely asserts. "I only ask one thing. Have all the Jews begin praying for me right away. I need all the help I can get."

Cut to Xerxes' outer office. Esther politely asks the secretary to buzz her in to see her husband. The secretary refuses her with a quiver in her voice. "He won't see anyone right now," she stutters. "In fact, his last words to me before he shut the door were that anyone who disturbed him would be shot!"

Esther bows her head for a moment, and a montage of praying Jews plays across the screen. She knows they're praying for her. She knows what God would have her do. She boldly steps to the door and reaches for the handle.

"No!" screams the secretary.

Inside Xerxes' lavishly appointed office, the door opens and Esther courageously steps across the threshold. There is a long, pregnant pause. Suddenly the voice of Xerxes cries out, "Esther! What a pleasant surprise! Are you going shopping? Do you need the credit card?"

"No, honey," she smiles, "I just wanted to see if you and Haman would come to a special dinner this evening. I've planned it just for you!"

"Of course, darling. We'll be there!"

Dinner that night is an extravagant feast with top-notch entertainment (Sinbad hosts, with musical appearances by Celine Dion, Kenny G, and Faith Hill). At the end of the evening, Esther asks the men to join her the next night for more festivities. They gladly agree.

Cut to Haman at the water cooler with his buddies the next morning, bragging about being the only person other than the king invited to Esther's party. But his excitement is dampened by the memory of his many run-ins with Esther's cousin, Mordecai.

"I've got it!" he exclaims with a cruel glint in his eye. "I'll build a huge gallows and get permission to hang that troublemaker Mordecai. I've got the king wrapped around my finger. I know he'll let me do it!" He picks up the phone and demands that a work crew get right on the task.

That evening, the party at Esther's is just as much fun as the night before, but it ends abruptly.

"What's up, Esther?" Xerxes asks.

The camera moves in for a closeup as she takes a deep breath. "Someone has sold out my people. We are going to be destroyed!"

"Who could do such a thing?" Xerxes thunders (apparently, he didn't know about her Jewish heritage).

With a dramatic fling of her wrist, Esther points to Haman. "It was him!"

Xerxes storms from the room in anger, and Haman throws himself at Esther's feet.

"Don't let him hurt me!" he pathetically whimpers.

Esther looks at him sadly. Xerxes returns and sees Haman grabbing for his wife. "Are you insane?" the king roars. "Are you going to molest my wife right in front of me?"

Just at that moment the king's cell phone rings.

"What?" he barks into the receiver.

"Sir, the gallows are ready."

"What gallows?"

"Isn't this Haman? Isn't this extension 354?"

"No, this is 364. But I'm interested in these gallows. Tell me about them."

The closing scenes show Haman hanging (I guess this cements a PG-13 rating), news reports of the Jewish extermination being cancelled, crowds celebrating, and Esther being hugged by Mordecai. A slow-motion shot captures Esther's beaming face as she looks to heaven and raises her hands in praise. Then the camera pulls back, and Xerxes comes and stands next to her. He puts his arm around her waist and looks up as well. Fade to the credits.

I know I've written this story as a movie, but I don't want us to forget that it really happened (with just a bit of literary license). Esther was a real woman with a powerful touch. She was given the opportunity to touch thousands of lives, literally saving them from death. But she had to have enough courage to risk her own life first—as well as enough wisdom to recognize she could never succeed on her own. She fasted and prayed and did everything she could to prepare herself. But she also enlisted all the Jews in the kingdom to fast and pray with her. She knew she needed the prayer support of others.

Are you like Esther? Do you take prayer seriously? Do you pray and seek the prayers of others before making important decisions or taking critical actions that will impact your life and the lives of those around you? We may never be asked to save an entire group of people like Esther was, but we might truly save lives if our words and actions lead people to a relationship with Jesus Christ—and those lives will be eternal!

We can't reach people and touch their lives for Christ on our own, however. We need God's help. We need to devote ourselves to prayer and ask others to join us. If you don't have a list of people you're praying for—people you know who need the touch of God in their lives— let me encourage you to stop and make one right now. Then find a few friends you can ask to pray with you on a regular basis.

And while you're praying for others, don't forget to pray for yourself. Pray that your actions will speak loudly for Christ. Pray that your words will lead others to Jesus. Pray that you'll have the strength to do and say what you know God has put in your heart—even if you face the risk of embarrassment, harassment, or persecution. Pray for the courage to touch others and for purity of heart as you do.

The truth is, real-life dramas are all around you. Real people are in need of God's love through your touch. You may not win any Oscars— but if you do your part, I promise God will applaud.

Lord, I love you. Now help me to love others enough to pray for them.

Devote yourselves to prayer, being watchful and thankful.
—Colossians 4:2

I do not want to dance beside the streams without you with me
Or see the angels fill the sky.
—Cindy Morgan, "Will You Be There?"

The Finishing Touch

We've covered a lot of ground as we've considered how women leave their fingerprints on the world. We've looked at women in the Bible and in history, as well as women who are alive today—women who are famous and women who aren't, women who've made the world a better place with their touch and women who've set such a bad example that they've shown us how *not* to touch the people around us. Their stories have moved us and taught us about the power of a woman's touch. They've reminded us that we, as women, have unique abilities and opportunities to impact the lives of others with the love of God.

I can think of many more stories I'd love to tell, and I bet you can think of some too. But we'll have to save them for another day. The time has come for the finishing touch.

What is the finishing touch? It's that one last swipe of the comb across my three-year-old niece's bangs after I've brushed her hair and turned her around to examine her. It's that blue pocket I took time to sew on my son's new bathrobe to make it "just perfect, Mom." It's that one last curlicue of frosting I squeezed onto the birthday cake to give it exactly the right flair. It's that final plump of the pillows on the sofa before the guests arrive. It's that last, lingering squeeze my husband gives me when he says good-bye. It's that special moment when we look at our handiwork and say, "It's finished."

Of course, if you're like me, you don't get to say those words very often. Someone once observed that a woman's work is never done—and judging from the mountain of clothes in my laundry room, the

191

stack of dishes in my sink, and the pile of books waiting to be shelved in my office, I'd have to agree!

Do we ever get to look at the fingerprints we've left on others and say, "It's finished"? Most of the time, no. The truth is, many of our touches will have to be repeated again and again before our fingerprints are set and dry. (Just think how many times a mother has to tell her children to wash their hands before dinner. Some touches take an eternity to become permanent!)

Other times, we only get one quick touch in someone's life, and then it really is finished—they move on, or we move on, and we don't get a chance to erase the touch and try again. That means we must be careful and purposeful with every touch we make. We never know if it's our finishing touch or not. Will this be the last time you see that person? Will this be the only chance you get to make a difference in his or her life? Even as I write this, Mike and Tony are walking out the door to run errands for me. Will I have a chance to touch them again? Only God knows.

I don't mean to sound morbid or create undue anxiety. But I do think we need a good kick in the pants sometimes to remind us that people won't wait forever. They need to be touched with God's love now. *Now.* Good intentions will never change lives. "I'll call and volunteer tomorrow." "I'll send that note next week." "I'm still a bit uncomfortable…I'll hug her next time." What are you waiting for? Will you have regrets if you wait? What if you miss the moment when your touch could have made all the difference?

Learning to touch is an ongoing process, and I admit I haven't mastered it yet. I can look back and remember many times my touch wasn't gentle, many times I should have reached out but didn't. Instead of wallowing in regret, however, I'm moving forward, looking for ways I can improve my relationship with God and with others. I'm actively looking for opportunities to reach out and touch people. I know I'm far from perfect, but that doesn't stop me from touching. My fingerprints are the marks of God's love, working through me. I want to see them all over the place.

I want to see your fingerprints all over the place too. After all, Jesus has touched our lives with such love, joy, mercy, and forgiveness. Let's go now and touch others—and point them to him.

The Finishing Touch

Lord, give me that loving "kick in the pants" to spur me on toward touching others. Use my fingerprints to spread your love to the world around me.

And let us consider how we may spur one another
on toward love and good deeds.
—Hebrews 10:24

Notes

Chapter One. Your Fingerprints Are All over the Place!

1. The facts on the Hiller story, the case of *People v. Jennings*, and the 1904 World's Fair were adapted from Mark A. Acree, *"People v. Jennings: A Significant Case in American Fingerprint History,"* MSFS, University of Alabama at Birmingham. Found on-line at: http://www.iinet.com/market/scafo/library/140401.html.

Chapter Two. He Touched Me

1. "Ten Differences Between Men and Women that Make a Difference in Women's Health," Society for Women's Health Research, Web site: www.womens-health.org/insertB.htm.

2. Ibid.

3. Adapted from "Gender Differences in Nonverbal Cues" on the academic home page of Donnell A. King, found on the Pellissippi State Technical Community College Web site at: www2.pstcc.cc.tn.us/~dking/nvcom2.htm. Copyright 1997, 1998, 1999 by Donnell A. King.

4. Ibid.

5. Ibid.

6. Ibid.

7. "Men and Women Have Different Kinds and Levels of Emotional Intelligence. EQ for Both Sexes Is Key to Workplace Success," from EQ and Gender (Toronto, Ontario, and Buffalo, New York), 15 August 1997. Found on-line at: www.pro-philes.com/researchGENDER.htm.

8. "How Different Are Men and Women?" Think Tank with Benn Wattenberg, radio airdate 14 July 1995. Transcript found on-line at: www.pbs.org/thinktank/archive/transcripts/transcript.216.html.

9. Taken from 1990 United States Census Bureau. Found on-line at: www.lifesmith.com/comnames.html.

10. Luke 1:28, 30.

11. Luke 1:38.

12. Luke 1:46–55.

13. See Ephesians 4:11–13; Romans 12:6–8; and 1 Corinthians 12: 7–11.

14. Ed German, "Latent Print Examination," September 1999. Found online at: http://onin.com/fp/lpfaq.html.

15. The full text of this story is found in Luke 17:11–19.

16. This story, including the quotes by Steven Curtis Chapman, are adapted from "Song by Song" from the press kit for his album *Dive* (Sparrow, 1999), and from "Steven Curtis Chapman: Finding Peace Amidst Confusion," *Living with Teenagers*, Lifeway Publishers, December 1999.

17. "Fingerprints of God" from Stephen Curtis Chapman and Scotty Smith, *Speechless* (Grand Rapids, Mich.: Zondervan), 153–54. Copyright 1999 by Steven Curtis Chapman and Scotty Smith. Used by permission.

Chapter Three. The Touch Treatment

1. Nina's sister, Wanda, has given me permission to tell this story and quote her.

2. "Selfless Organ Donor Relies on Her Faith," *The Reporter-Herald* (Loveland, Colo.), 23 October 1999.

3. Adapted from the Alberta, Canada, Scoutbook (Northern Region) found at the Canadian Scouting Web address: http://www.interlog.com/~speirs/spirit/spir0037.htm.

4. See the World Hug Week Web site at: http://oac3.hsc.uth.tmc.edu/~bardoin/hugs/

5. Read the whole passage in Isaiah 11:1–9.

6. 2 Kings 5:3.

7. This story is found in 2 Kings 5:1–15.

8. The story is adapted from Linda Carlson Johnson, *Mother Teresa: Protector of the Sick* (Woodbridge, Conn.: Blackbirch Press, Inc., 1991), 6–10.

9. Ibid., 50.

10. Jose Luis Gonzalez-Balado, compiler, *Mother Teresa: In My Own Words* (Liguori, Mo.: Liguori Publications, 1996), 26.

11. Jose Luis Gonzalez-Balado, editor, *Loving Jesus* (Ann Arbor, Mich.: Servant Publications, 1991), 21.

12. Ibid., 35.

13. Becky Benenate and Joseph Durepos, editors, *No Greater Love* (Novato, Calif.: New World Library, 1997), 56.

14. Mother Teresa, "Daily Prayer: Jesus My Patient," from Malcolm Muggeridge, *Something Beautiful for God: Mother Teresa of Calcutta* (San

Francisco: Harper, 1986). As quoted on the Web site: http://agelessinitiatives. com/inspire/moteresa.htm.

Chapter Four. As Good As New

1. The story of the woman at the well is found in John 4:4–42.

2. Adapted from Mike Nappa and Dr. Norm Wakefield, "Laughing Matters," from *True Stories of Transformed Lives* (Wheaton, Ill.: Tyndale, 1999), 71–72.

3. The story of the Anglin family is adapted from Patty Anglin with Joe Musser, *Acres of Hope* (Uhrichsville, Ohio: Promise Press, 1999).

4. The quotes by Helen Keller in this chapter, along with the details of her life story, are taken from Helen Keller, *The Story of My Life* (New York: Bantam Books, 1990).

5. William J. Bennett, editor, *The Book of Virtues*, "Helen Keller and Anne Sullivan" (New York: Simon & Schuster, 1993).

Chapter Five. A Gentle Touch

1. "Dear Abby," *The Reporter-Herald* (Loveland, Colo.), 20 October 1999.

2. Abigail's story is found in 1 Samuel 25:1–44.

3. From the home page of "A Modern Herbal" by Mrs. M. Grieve, originally published in 1931, found on-line at: www.Botanical.com.

4. As excerpted under fair use laws from *The Book of Wisdom*, (Sisters, Ore.: Multnomah, 1997), 550.

Chapter Six. Home, Sweet Home

1. The stories of Shawn, Michelle, and Starr are from Toni Locy, "Like Mother, Like Daughter?" *U.S. News and World Report* , 4 October 1999. This article can be found on-line at: http://www.usnews.com/usnews/issue/ 991004/prison.htm.

2. Ibid.

3. Source unknown.

Chapter Seven. Won't You Be My Neighbor?

1. Rene Jones is a friend who has agreed to share her story.

2. Matthew 19:14.

3. Andrea Rozum, "I Am," copyright 1999. Reprinted with permission.

4. Ann Marie Rozum is a friend who, along with her daughter, gave permission to have their story told.

5. "Women Who Make a Difference," *Family Circle Magazine*, 15 July 1997.

6. Source unknown.

7. Judy Harper Spaar, *Thanks for Being My Friend* (Kansas City, Mo.: Andrews McMeel Publishing, 1999), 188, 192, 213, 235, 258, 294.

8. 2 Corinthians 5:20.

9. John 14:6, italics added.

10. James 3:6, 8.

11. Read James 1:19.

Chapter Eight. The Hands of God

1. For more information about starting or becoming involved in a prison ministry, contact Prison Fellowship, P.O. Box 17500, Washington, D.C., 20041-0500. Or visit their Web site: www.prisonfellowship.org.

2. Matthew 10:41.

Chapter Nine. Touch and Go

1. Quotes from Robin Jones-Gunn and information regarding her life are drawn from my friendship and correspondence with her.

2. Source unknown.

3. Romans 16:16; 1 Corinthians 16:20; 2 Corinthians 13:12; 1 Thessalonians 5:26; 1 Peter 5:14.

4. Mark 12:43–44.

5. John 12:6.

6. This story is adapted from Barbara Johnson, *He's Gonna Toot and I'm Gonna Scoot* (Nashville, Tenn.: Word, 1999), 142–49.

7. "Splashes of Joy," *USA Today*, 15 December 1999.

8. See Genesis 1:1–26; John 1:1–14; and James 3:1–12.

Chapter Ten. I'm Touched

1. Lauren Gelfand, "Charity Out of Tragedy," *The Reporter-Herald* (Loveland, Colo.), 14 December 1999.

2. Luke 10:41–42.

3. 1 Corinthians 13:1–3.